-dedication-

*For Philip, Saffron, Imogen, and
Penelope—who have who have
watched me bloom, wilt, and bloom again
and continue to love me through it.*

*To the memory of my college advisor
Shirley Shedd, whose belief in my potential as
a young journalist planted seeds of confidence
that continue to bloom long after she's gone—
her legacy lives on through each student she
encouraged, including me, proving that when
we speak life into others, our impact outlives us.*

*For my messy bun and stretch pants tribe—
the flowers in my bouquet who embrace all my
authentic quirks and love me because of them.*

*For all who find themselves pushing
through pavement, reaching for the light: May
you find your way to bloom, not despite your
circumstances, but through them.
You are seen. You are known. You are
completely loved. You are never alone.*

*For the Master Gardener, who sees beauty
in the wildflowers and purpose in the weeds.
You lavish me with good things.*

*To my Great Pyrenees pups Stanley and
Stuart—you are my everyday
God-sent dandelion fluff.*

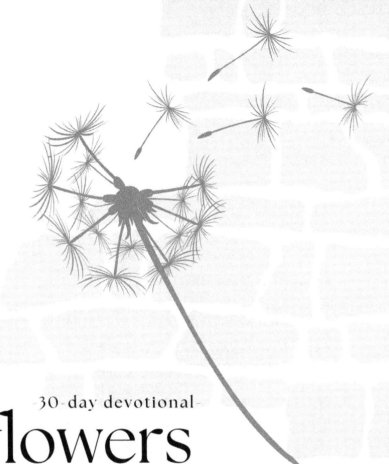

-30-day devotional-

flowers
find a way

*Resilient Blooms Rooted
in Relentless Faith*

amber weigand buckley

#barefacedcreativemedia | springfield, missouri | 65802

contents

God over every
sprout of promise
over unexpected weeds
that bloom
beautiful purple flowers
i'm going to trust you
to do only what you can do
because that's what you've done
through all my yesterdays
and what you've written out
in the promises
of all of my tomorrows

#barefacedjournals

-introduction-
a legacy in petals

I find myself staring at every flower I find in concrete, wondering what stories it could tell. What elements did it have to push through to get to where it is now? How can some of them keep standing tall right in the middle of the road, not even flinching with the zoom of the traffic?

There's something almost defiant about it—this fragile wisp of life breaking through what should be impenetrable. It's amazing that it keeps its softness no matter how much resistance it has come against in its short life. It doesn't ask permission.

It doesn't wait for perfect conditions. It simply finds a crack, a sliver of possibility, and reaches for the light.

This collection of my reflection moments, much like those haphazard flowers, isn't filled with polished, perfect spiritual insights. These devotions were born from pictures that continue to hold my memory— experiences I've walked through that rooted something stronger in me. Throughout, I'm including some of my journal moments, poems, and verses—raw seeds of my conversations with God that helped me realize there was potential behind adversity. They weren't written from a place of having it all figured out, but from conversations between me—a perfectly imperfect barefacedgirl and the God who loves me.

I've never been good at keeping up appearances. The makeup, the masks, the pretending—it's exhausting. And honestly? God doesn't need me to be polished.

He meets me in my barefaced moments, when I'm completely unfiltered, without pretense. Just me and Him, authentic and real.

My journey with mental health through ministry disappointments, family struggles, and spiritual doubts has taught me this: flowers find a way. Not because they're stronger than concrete, but because they're persistent. They keep reaching, keep growing, keep seeking the light until they see a way to the surface and take a leap in that direction. You won't find three easy steps to a perfect faith here.

These are honest reflections from someone who has felt the weight of the concrete and decided to bloom anyway.

Someone who has discovered that God doesn't just meet us in our strength but grows His strength through our weakness. He wants us to give Him a chance to do just that. You will also find some intentional and unintentional typos, so it will be like a scavenger hunt of imperfect words coming from a perfectly imperfect girl—and in many ways probably a lot like you.

I've divided these devotions into four paths we all walk in our spiritual journey:

Pushing Through Pavement — When life feels like it's buried you under a parking lot of problems, God gives us the stubborn hope to keep pushing upward.
Revived from the Root Up — Getting honest about what feeds our souls and having the courage to cut away the stuff that's just taking up space.

Soaking Up the Sun — Real talk about life struggles, especially the times when God feels a million miles away—but isn't.

Wildflowers Need to Wander — Embracing fresh callings, unexpected joy, and the beautiful ways God transforms our journey.

So, whether you're feeling buried or beginning to break through, I invite you to join me in these reflections. Let's cultivate relentless faith together, one resilient bloom at a time.

-section one-

CULTIVATING
DETERMINED BLOOMS

pushing through
pavement

*When circumstances seems
impossible to break through, God
gives us the persistence to push
upward toward His light.*

i love to stop
and watch the petals
pushing their way
through the pavement
their silent persistence
pulls forward my footing
as that is the
working of flowers
#barefacedjournals

the defiance of holy blooms

**The light shines in the darkness,
and the darkness has not overcome it.
—John 1:5 (NIV)**

I'm pretty sure I have dandelion DNA, as I've always
been drawn to these persistent blooms simply because
they refuse to stay where they're told. Maybe it's
because I know what it feels like to be pushed into the
corner, overlooked, and labeled as something that is
too flawed or "out there" to be acceptable. Or maybe it's
because I recognize and relate to the holy defiance in
their journey—pushing through darkness toward light,
no matter the cost.

*No matter what others may see whether they judge the
blooms as worthy or not. All that yellow headstrong
beauty is pushed out through its boldness to overcome.*

This is why I love to stop and look at blooms pushing
their way through the pavement. Their silent
persistence inspires my own journey forward, as
witnessing determination in nature strengthens my own
resolve.

*I've spent most of my life searching for cracks—those
narrow spaces where light filters through darkness.*

When I face resistance or darkness, I intentionally look
upward toward the light I know is there. This deliberate
focus on hope encourages me to lift my head even in the

most confining, challenging situations. And beautiful girl, I want you to understand this truth, too.

> *Breaking is the essential life spark*
> *—the birthplace for any seed that blooms.*

Those breaking periods, no matter if it is a mess of my own making, that's were I should take , not shame, because that's where Father's light shines the brightest. That's where he wants to shine—through our humanness.

Martin Luther King Jr. once said, "If you can't fly, then run; if you can't run, then walk; if you can't walk, then crawl, but whatever you do, you have to keep moving forward." Those flowers that don't give up when they hit resistance—they adapt, finding another route, another crack, another possibility.

Like the nature of the bones and dirt of the human condition, we aren't meant to be perfect. We're made to be real—cracked, broken vessels that somehow still hold the light. And in that beautiful contradiction lies our greatest purpose: to be so authentically ourselves, so honestly broken, that when God's light shines through us, no one mistakes the source of the glow.

This truth becomes most visible to me when I encounter wildflowers growing in impossible places—between sidewalk cracks, in the gravel by railroad tracks, or through a tiny opening in a rock face. These aren't carefully cultivated garden blooms with ideal soil and regular watering. These are determined little warriors, making beauty where beauty shouldn't be possible. Their persistence reminds me that God specializes in bringing life to the most barren places.

> *The flower doesn't breakthrough because it*
> *has some special superpower—it breaks through because*
> *it simply cannot help but reach for the light.*

That's what it was made for. That's what we were made for too. This divine design within us reflects the truth that John's gospel articulates so beautifully: the light always shines in the darkness, and the darkness has never been able to extinguish it. No matter how hot the concrete, how heavy the burden, light finds a way to break through.

This is the story God has been writing since creation —light speaking into darkness, life emerging from void, order from chaos. He continues to write this story in our lives. When we face our own concrete barriers — the diagnoses, the losses, the rejections, the disappointments—we carry within us the same divine DNA that says, "Reach for the light anyway."

So, when you're feeling buried under the weight of expectations, crushed by circumstances beyond your control, remember the dandelion. Remember its holy defiance, its silent persistence. And know that you, too, can push through what seems impenetrable, not because you're stronger than your obstacles, but because you were designed to seek the light.

The concrete doesn't stand a chance against
a flower that refuses to stay buried.

And neither do your circumstances when you let your soul do what it was created to do—reach persistently, defiantly, hopefully toward the God who made you.

Prayer: Father, thank you for your light always shining in the darkness that cannot be overcome. Help me to embrace the holy defiance of a flower breaking through concrete—not because I'm stronger than my obstacles, but because I'm drawn to your light. When I feel overlooked or pushed aside, remind me that darkness has no power over the light you've placed within me. In Jesus's name, Amen.

growing forward

Tending the Soil
Where in your life do you feel like you're pushing through concrete right now?

When have you witnessed "holy defiance" in someone else's life? What impact did it have on you?

How has God's light reached you in your darkest moments?

Sowing the Seed
Find a flower growing in an unlikely place today (through concrete, in a rocky area, etc.). Take a photo or simply pause to observe it. Let it remind you of your own capacity to reach for light in difficult circumstances.

Rooting in Truth
The light shines in the darkness, and the darkness has not overcome it. —John 1:5 (NIV)

Branching Out
Romans 5:3-5, James 1:2-4, Psalm 18:28-29

seeds of thought

i watch snowflakes gather
on greens that will never fall
convenient vines that
will never need tending
or the refreshment of rain
which pools on their leaves
their concealed half-truths
are apparent in the closer view
they may not get eaten by bugs
but their leaves are ripe in fray
#barefacedjournals

-day two-
a paradise made in plastic

People look at the outward appearance, but the LORD looks at the heart.— 1 Samuel 16:7 (NIV)

I have a confession that might get my gardening credentials permanently revoked (if I had any to begin with): I've decorated my yard with plastic greenery. Yes, you read that right. Artificial, never-need-watering, forever-green fake ivy hanging around my chill space in the backyard, complemented by fake Ficus trees and plastic hanging plants from Temu and Dollar Tree. My reasoning was bulletproof—I kill plants with the efficiency of a frost in April. I've murdered more greenery than I care to admit, and frankly, my thumbs are about as far from green as you can get.

My plastic ivy looked perfect at first. Perpetually verdant. No watering, no weeding, no wilting.

My backyard chill space looked magazine-worthy with minimal effort—until winter came.

There's something deeply unsettling about seeing bright green ivy peeking through January snow. While every authentic plant in the neighborhood had gracefully entered its seasonal sleep, my artificial greenery stood in defiant denial of winter's reality, creating this bizarre time-warp effect that made visitors do double-takes. It looked...wrong. Like spiritual plastic surgery gone bad. Like I was trying to force summer's smile onto winter's face.

I've thought about taking them down for winter, but honestly, who has the time? And why waste the money replacing them when they still look mostly decent? Besides, they're in the backyard where only friends and family see them—it's not like I'm putting on a show for the whole neighborhood.

Now, I should mention that my mom is the one who plants silk flowers in her window boxes. At least I have standards—I only go for green! But watching those plastic greens in my yard made me think about how we all try to maintain appearances in different ways.

Authentic faith embraces seasons. It acknowledges that dormancy is not death—it's preparation. That barrenness often precedes abundance. That the stripping away makes room for new growth.

I spent too much of my life concerned about saying the right thing—speaking fluent "Christianese."

There's something tempting about mastering the proper spiritual vocabulary, nodding along at just the right moments, quoting Scripture with perfect timing. It's like installing plastic plants—low maintenance, always looks right, never messy.

The thing about plastic plants is they might fool people from a distance, but up close, they're obviously artificial. They may look nice initially, but they're missing something essential—life.

They don't grow, change, adapt, or participate in the greater ecosystem. They take nothing in and give nothing back. They simply...exist, static and unchanging.

I worry sometimes that my faith has plastic moments—when I'm tempted to say the "right" people-pleasing spiritual things instead of my messy, authentic truth—where I am in the moment. "The bless God, everything is wonderful in my life" on repeat. It's so easy to fall into this pattern without even realizing it. The church world can subtly pressure us to present perpetually polished spiritual lives rather than reveal the complicated reality of our faith journeys with all their ups and downs.

But here's what I'm learning: God isn't interested in my plastic perfection. He's after authentic transformation—the kind that requires seasons of both visible growth and hidden renewal.

The kind that sometimes means standing empty-handed and bare-souled before Him, trusting that this season of apparent barrenness is preparation for new blooming. Paul understood this when he wrote to the Philippians about being content in every situation—whether well-fed or hungry, whether living in plenty or in want (Philippians 4:12). He wasn't advocating for a plastic smile regardless of circumstances. He was describing an authentic faith that acknowledges seasons while trusting the Gardener's perfect timing.

So, this spring I'm trying my hand at planting some real plants in the flower bed. Yes, they die back in winter. Yes, sometimes they fail to thrive despite my best efforts.

Yes, they require more work and bring more disappointment. But they're real. They participate in the authentic rhythm of creation. They take in what's harmful and release what brings life. They drop seeds that promise future beauty.

And in their realness, even in their dormancy, they reflect something true about the God who created both winter and spring, both growth and rest, both blooming and pruning.

Prayer: Father, forgive me for the plastic places of what I should say faith—where I've chosen the appearance of perfection over the reality of process. Help me embrace spiritual seasons with honesty and trust, knowing that both the visible growth of spring and the hidden renewal of winter are part of your design. Teach me to value authenticity over appearance, truth over pretense. I want my life to be genuinely rooted in you, not artificially anchored in others' approval. I trust your timing, your nurturing, and your perfect plan for genuine fruitfulness in my life. In Jesus's name, Amen.

growing forward

Tending the Soil
In what areas of your life have you been presenting a "plastic" version of yourself rather than embracing authenticity?

What spiritual "seasons" are you currently resisting or trying to skip past?

How might your current season of dormancy or struggle actually be preparing you for future growth?

Sowing the Seed
Find an area of your life where you've been maintaining appearances. Take one small step toward authenticity this week—perhaps by sharing a genuine struggle with a trusted friend or acknowledging a difficult season to yourself in prayer.

Rooting in Truth
People look at the outward appearance, but the LORD looks at the heart. —1 Samuel 16:7 (NIV)

Branching Out
Ecclesiastes 3:1-8, Philippians 4:11-13, 2 Corinthians 4:16-18

seeds of thought

seeds of thought

i will turn my face
towards the sun
and cup the rain for the
softening of petals
#barefacedjournals

-day three-
the strength of softness

"He will not break a bruised reed, and he will not put out a smoldering wick." —Matthew 12:20 (CSB)

Have you ever felt like you needed to grow a harder shell just to make it through this world? I've been there—thinking I needed to somehow get tougher to do business in spaces traditionally dominated by men. The subtle message that my natural softness was a liability haunted me.

I remember walking into important meetings and consciously lowering my voice, minimizing my emotional responses, trying to embody what I thought was 'strength.' I'd come home exhausted from the performance, feeling like I'd betrayed something essential about who God created me to be.

One day, while watching dandelion seeds float through the air—so delicate yet traveling for miles—I had a revelation. Those seeds weren't surviving despite their softness—they were thriving because of it. Their gentle flexibility allowed them to travel farther than any hard-shelled seed ever could.

I realized I'd completely misunderstood strength.

Real strength isn't about becoming harder or rougher. It's not about developing thicker skin or sharper elbows.

True strength—God's kind of strength—often looks like remaining soft even when you have been crushed underfoot over and over.

It looks like Jesus, who wept openly and wasn't afraid to show compassion. There's something profoundly subversive about maintaining your softness in spaces that demand hardness.

It's a quiet rebellion that says, "I will not become what crushes me. I will remain exactly as God created me to be—and still find a way forward."

The feminine mystics of church history understood this. Women like Julian of Norwich, Teresa of Avila, and Hildegard of Bingen didn't achieve their profound spiritual insights by rejecting their feminine nature. They embraced it fully, finding in their womanhood a unique path to understanding God's heart.

Teresa of Avila once wrote, "The important thing is not to think much but to love much."

This is the wisdom of softness speaking—knowing that sometimes the path forward isn't through force but through love, not through hardness but through heart. And I'm learning that my strength doesn't come from becoming something I'm not. It comes from fully embracing who God created me to be.

Like those feathery dandelion seeds, I don't have to become hardened to travel far. My softness—my emotional intelligence, my intuition, my capacity for empathy—these aren't weaknesses to overcome. They're God-given strengths to cultivate.

So if you've felt the pressure to harden yourself to survive, remember: the God who made you celebrates your softness. The Creator who designed seeds to float on gentle breezes, without losing their ability to take root and grow into something beautiful, sees your sensitivity as strength, not weakness.

> *Stay soft in a world that tries to harden you.*
> *It's not a liability; it's a divine gift to be cultivated.*

It's not your weakness; it's precisely where God's strength is made perfect."

Prayer: Father God, thank you for creating me with a sensitivity that reflects your heart. Forgive me for the times I've believed the lie that I need to harden myself to be effective in this world. Help me to see how Jesus modeled true strength through His compassion, tears, and gentle touch. Remind me that I don't need to become like concrete to break through concrete—I can remain authentically who you made me to be and still accomplish mighty things. Show me how my softness can become a revolutionary force in a world that values hardness. In Jesus's name, Amen.

growing forward

Tending the Soil
Where have you felt pressure to "toughen up" in your life, particularly in a way that felt unnatural to your God-given personality?

Think of a time when your gentleness or sensitivity became a strength rather than a weakness. What happened?

What would it look like to embrace your God-given softness while still maintaining healthy boundaries?

Sowing the Seed
Notice when you naturally respond with softness (empathy, compassion, patience) this week. Instead of judging that response as weakness, thank God for it as a reflection of His heart working through you.

Rooting in Truth
"He will not break a bruised reed, and he will not put out a smoldering wick." —Matthew 12:20 (CSB)

Branching Out
Matthew 5:5, 2 Corinthians 12:9-10, Galatians 5:22-23

seeds of thought

carry me beyond
the learned sickness of patterns
to plant fresh gardens
and hope-filled dreams
breaking family lines
that tore me at the seams
my story rides a new breeze
with a heart that whispers
this ends with me
#barefacedjournals

-day four-
any way the wind blows

"The wind blows where it wishes, and you hear its sound, but you do not know where it comes from or where it goes. So, it is with everyone who is born of the Spirit." — John 3:8 (ESV)

I never had allergies growing up in Ozark Mountain Country. But after living in London for a while and then coming back home? Whew! The sneezing, burning eyes, itchy ears—it's like my body forgot how to handle good ol' American pollen. And it's only gotten worse with age. I'm basically a walking pollen detector now. Some people have superpowers—I have seasonal suffering.

You know what's crazy though? This stuff that makes me miserable is incredible. Pollen is like nature's FedEx—tiny little packages carrying genetic messages across miles and miles. And here's the kicker—the very stuff that makes me sneeze can help build immunity if you're exposed to it in the right way.

The potential for immunity comes from confronting these irritants through consistent regular exposures, which can make you stronger and more resistant to them.

That got me thinking about the invisible things we carry around. Not just eye color or height that we inherit, but those family patterns that nobody talks about.

The way your grandpa handled stress somehow shows up in how you handle it too. The fears your mom carried that now live rent-free in your head.

Some of these messages take generations to fully land. Like those seeds that drift in the wind for miles before finding the perfect spot to grow. Sometimes the pain our parents or grandparents couldn't face finds its way to us, looking for someone to finally deal with it. But here's the good news—not all inherited stuff gets to keep growing. Some seeds run smack into God's grace.

Some family patterns that have been running for generations suddenly hit a wall because someone (maybe you!) finally said, "This stops with me."

It reminds me of what Paul said in 2 Corinthians about looking at what can't be seen. The visible stuff—that's temporary. It's the invisible things that last forever. God's work, much like pollen, is often invisible but incredibly powerful.

I don't know about you, but I've spent way too much time fixated on the obvious, loud, dramatic stuff in my life. But the real healing? It happens quietly. Persistently. Like how a single grain of pollen can travel miles to create new life.

Just like my body can learn to handle pollen better through exposure over time, our hearts can learn new responses to old triggers through God's healing.

The family pattern that used to send you spiraling? With enough exposure to God's truth, it might just become the very thing that sends you straight to prayer instead.

When Jesus talked to Nicodemus about Holy Spirit, He compared it to the wind. You can't see it, but boy, you sure can see what it does. You can feel its effects.

That's how God works in our lives too—invisible but undeniable.

So, if you're carrying something heavy today—some invisible burden passed down or picked up along the way—remember that God specializes in rewriting those stories. He's the ultimate genetic engineer, capable of transforming what hurts into what heals.

Trust the journey, friend. Trust that healing can be as persistent as those pollen grains that find their way through the tiniest air gaps. The invisible carriers of God's love and grace are constantly at work, even when your spiritual sinuses are all stuffed up.

Prayer: God, sometimes the invisible stuff I'm carrying feels heavier than anything I can see. Help me trust your healing process, even when it makes me uncomfortable like pollen season. Transform the patterns that don't serve your purpose in my life. Help me be open to your wind, your movement, your rearranging of what I've always known. And when I start sneezing at change, remind me that sometimes discomfort is just part of building immunity to old ways. In Jesus's name, Amen.

growing forward

Tending the Soil
What family patterns—positive or negative—do you see
repeating in your own life?

How might God be using your discomfort to build
spiritual immunity?

What invisible work might God be doing in your life
right now?

Sowing the Seed
Write down one family pattern you want to break. Then
write "This ends with me" and place it somewhere
you'll see it daily as a reminder of your commitment to
change.

Rooting in Truth
The wind blows where it wishes, and you hear its
sound, but you do not know where it comes from or
where it goes. So, it is with everyone who is born of the
Spirit. —John 3:8 (ESV)

Branching Out
Ezekiel 18:19-20, 2 Corinthians 5:17, Isaiah 43:18-19

seeds of thought

isn't the bud
just as beautiful as the
bloom in the way it holds
the rain and the leaf
as well the branch it finds
its great unfolding through
the loveliness of each root
that in the earth's care
holds the bouquet together
#barefacedjournals

-day five-
all leaves. no bloom.

A generous person will prosper; whoever refreshes others will be refreshed. — Proverbs 11:25 (NIV)

Every spring, my yard taunts me with what might have been. Dozens of daffodil leaves push hopefully through the soil, standing tall and green with promise. But year after year, the same disappointing result—all leaves, no bloom. These determined little soldiers have been marching up faithfully each spring since we moved in, but after a couple promising years when we first arrived some 26 years ago, the flowers never followed again.

My mother-in-law revealed a fact that was the source of the problem: "They're too crowded. They need space to bloom."

Apparently, when daffodil bulbs multiply underground over decades, they need to be divided, or they'll compete for the same resources. Without enough space for each plant to access what it needs; they can still produce leaves but lack the nutrients to create flowers. They're surviving, but not thriving—existing, but not blooming.

I stood staring at my flowerless leaves, hearing God's gentle whisper: "This is how you have learned to live— by doing as much as possible in every spare minute you have."

That hurt, but it was undeniably true.

How often do I pack my life so full that I have no space

to truly bloom? How frequently do I crowd my days with so many commitments, activities, and distractions that I have just enough energy to stand upright, but not enough to flourish?

*I'm producing leaves without flowers—
going through the motions of growth without
experiencing the beauty of full flourishing.*

Jesus understood this need for space. We see Him repeatedly withdrawing to quiet places to pray and be alone with the Father. Even with people clamoring for His attention, with needs pressing in from every side, He recognized that without that vital space for communion with God, His ministry would be all leaves and no bloom.

"Very early in the morning, while it was still dark, Jesus got up, left the house and went off to a solitary place, where he prayed" (Mark 1:35, NIV). Not because He was avoiding responsibility, but because He understood that true fruitfulness requires intentional space.

*I'm learning that saying "no" can be a spiritual
practice as holy as saying "yes." That creating margins
in my life isn't selfish—it's stewardship.*

That sometimes the most productive thing I can do is to create space for God to work in and through me.

The irony of my crowded daffodils is that dividing them—which feels counterintuitive, like reducing them—leads to more abundant blooming. Sometimes our greatest growth comes from dividing our energies more intentionally, not from trying to do more.

In John 15, Jesus tells us He is the vine, and we are the branches. The vinedresser removes some branches and cultivates others—not to harm them, but to help them bear more fruit. Creating space—the intentional removal of what's excessive—allows for greater fruitfulness. What feels like loss becomes the pathway to abundance.

So, I've marked my calendar to divide those daffodil bulbs this fall, even if in my far-from green-thumb happens to kill them. To dig them up, separate them, and give each one room to access what it needs to not just grow, but bloom. After 26 years of waiting, it's time for action. And I'm asking God to show me what needs dividing in my life as well.

Where have I allowed good things to become too crowded? Where am I producing leaves without flowers? What needs to be cleared away so I can truly flourish?

Maybe you're feeling it too—that sense of being all leaves and no bloom. Going through the motions but missing the joy. Standing upright but not flourishing. If so, perhaps it's time to create some holy space in your life. To dig up what's been overcrowded for far too long and intentionally replant with room to thrive.

Because God hasn't called us to a life of just leaves. He's designed us for full flowering—that not only brings us joy but refreshes everyone around us. And that kind of blooming requires space.

Prayer: Father, forgive me for the times I've crowded my life so full that I have no space to truly bloom. Help me recognize where I need to create margins, where I need to divide what's become too dense, where I need to say "no" so I can fully say "yes" to what you're growing in me. Show me how to clear away what's excessive so I can bear fruit that lasts. I don't want to be all leaves and no bloom—I want my life to display the full flowering of your Spirit's work in me. Teach me the sacred practice of creating space for you to work. In Jesus's name, Amen.

growing forward

Tending the Soil
1. What areas of your life feel overcrowded right now, leaving you with "all leaves, no bloom?"

2. Where have you been saying "yes" when your spirit needs you to say "no?"

3. What specific activities or commitments might need to be "divided" or reduced to create more space for flourishing?

Sowing the Seed
Choose one area of your life that feels overcrowded. This week, intentionally create margin in that area— whether by declining a request, scheduling downtime, or removing something from your calendar. Notice how this intentional space affects your spiritual and emotional well-being.

Rooting in Truth
A generous person will prosper; whoever refreshes others will be refreshed. —Proverbs 11:25 (NIV)

Branching Out
Mark 1:35-37, John 15:1-5, Psalm 46:10

seeds of thought

i will not allow
the hate or
judgment
of others
overwrite my love
disrupt my peace
or replace my joy
in this life
#barefacedjournals

the toxic garden of approval

"Am I now trying to win the approval of human beings, or of God?" —Galatians 1:10 (NIV)

There's a garden in England where beauty is a deadly invitation. The Poison Garden at Alnwick Castle grows some of the world's most lethal plants—each bloom a masterpiece of deception. Visitors are warned not to touch, not even to breathe near certain specimens. Hemlock, foxglove, nightshade—stunning plants that carry death within their delicate petals.

I've cultivated my own version of this garden for years. Not with actual plants, but with expectations. Carefully tended hopes. Meticulously pruned performances. Each one looking perfect from the outside, while slowly choking out my true self.

I always said that I learned to lie in church. It sounds harsh, but it's true. I was more concerned with how people viewed me as a Christian leader than how God viewed me—even though deep down I knew He loved me regardless. I wasn't trying to impress anyone. I just wanted to be accepted at the table of leadership.

I spent years perfecting this dangerous landscape—cultivating not what would nourish my soul, but what would yield the praise and acceptance of others.

Each expectation was another layer of poison slowly suffocating my authentic spirit. I pruned away anything that didn't fit the mold. Shaped myself into something that looked impressive but couldn't truly thrive.

I didn't realize my mental health was deteriorating under the weight of all these expectations until I found myself standing on the edge of a Colorado mountain, wondering if my life even mattered anymore. That's when I realized the desire for approval could have literally taken me out.

> *You see, is simply filling your garden with "beautiful poison."*

It might look beautiful for a while, but eventually, it strips the health of anyone who comes in contact with those plants.

God didn't create us to fit into everyone else's vision of the perfect garden. In fact, many of those purple wildflowers that grow in my yard—ones many see as weeds—bring me such joy. To me, I don't care what they're called. I delight in them painting my landscape purple.

For me, the "purple weeds" that had emerged from this journey has helped me the world differently. I write better because I write from the depths of who I am. This journey has taken me to a place of authentic influence—becoming who I was divinely created to be rather than who others expected me to be.

When we stop tending the toxic garden of approval, we make room for authentic growth and genuine connection with God and others.

Prayer: Father, I've been tending a poison garden that's been killing my spirit. Help me uproot these toxic expectations with seeds of truth. Give me courage to let my garden gro w wild and authentic, filled with the purple blooms of genuine faith rather than the deadly flowers of performance. Lead me back to the place where my relationships flow from who I truly am, not who I think others want me to be. In Jesus's name, Amen.

growing forward

Tending the Soil
What specific expectations or "toxic flowers" have you been cultivating to gain others' approval?

How has your pursuit of approval affected your mental, emotional, and spiritual health?

What would your "garden" look like if you cultivated it for God's delight rather than human approval?

Sowing the Seed
Identify one area where you've been maintaining appearances for others. This week, practice authenticity in that area—not by being deliberately provocative, but by simply being honest about where you are and what you need.

Rooting in Truth
Am I now trying to win the approval of human beings, or of God? —Galatians 1:10 (NIV)

Branching Out
1 Samuel 16:7, John 8:32, Ephesians 2:10

seeds of thought

seeds of thought

do not be reckless
with the ones who
water your soul
fence their love
upend the thistles
that choke out
this sacred space
as we take joy
in watching each other rise
to meet the challenge
of each new day
together
#barefacedjournals

-day seven-
boundaries, not barbed wire

But the wisdom that comes from heaven is first of all pure; then peace-loving, considerate, submissive, full of mercy and good fruit, impartial and sincere.
—James 3:17 (NIV)

I'm gonna be honest. I have this little voice in my head sometimes that says, "You better get them before they get you." That competitive streak that whispers, "Someone's gonna beat you to the punch" or "They're stealing your idea!" You know what I'm talking about?

The business world basically tells us we should be the B-word to get ahead. Be cutthroat. Step on whoever's in your way. But there's this fine line between standing up for yourself and becoming someone who's hard and cunning—someone who slashes others off the trail.

> *In God's garden there's a difference between protective thorns and invasive thistles.*

Think about it: rose bushes have thorns, right? Those thorns aren't there to attack; they're there to protect something beautiful. But then there are thistles that spread everywhere, choking out everything around them just to claim more territory.

I remember sitting in meetings, feeling like someone was replicating what I was doing or saying, and that feeling of my stomach tense up. My first instinct was to get defensive—to mark my territory and make sure everyone knew that it was MY idea, MY project, MY ministry. I had to ask myself: is that really standing up for myself, or is that just me feeling threatened?

What's interesting is that God designed His garden with incredible diversity AND repetition. Have you noticed how many different varieties of daisies there are? They're all technically daisies, but each one has its unique characteristics. God didn't plant just one daisy and say, "Nobody else better grow anything that looks like this!"

> *When we plant boundaries instead of barbed wire, we create space for everyone to geniunely bloom.*

Let me tell you, I've had pretty much the premise to my book read back to me in different ways, and I've thought, "I hope you don't write a book about that!" But then I've tried to see those moments not as competition but as confirmation. God gives the same word to a lot of people. I mean, that's the nature of the Bible—He repeats himself quite a bit, even in one book!

The difference between standing up for yourself and being mean comes down to this: Are you protecting what's yours or are you trying to prevent someone else from having theirs?

Boundaries sound like: "This is my work, and I'm proud of it." Mean girl tactics sound like: "This is my work, and no one else better try anything similar."

Boundaries are like garden fences—they define space but still let the sunshine through. Meanness is like covering your garden in black tarp so no one else can see what you're growing.

> *Your unique garden doesn't need to be the only one on the block to be valuable.*

I know that when I've been hurt by others in this area, I've sometimes wanted to throw down and get them before they got me. However, as I was mulling over frustration this realization popped front and center of my mind: Sometimes we project what we're really thinking onto someone else to make ourselves feel better about our approach.

God isn't into photocopying—He's into unique creation. That's why He's created us to be individual beings.

But I also get it, you're gonna have similarities to someone out there. And instead of kicking back, maybe we should see that as our posse. I love it when I get into a group of women and find out we vibe on some area. It's energizing to find your people!

Standing up for yourself should never require tearing someone else down.

Just like in a garden, the strongest plants don't need to choke out others to thrive—they just need good roots, proper care, and the right amount of sunshine.

When I feel that step on my toe—that moment someone seems to be encroaching on "my territory"—I try to ask myself, "Why am I feeling this exactly? And what do I do with this feeling?" Sometimes in the process, I find out maybe there is a valid reason. Maybe we should moreover seek to have a conversation about an issue than to automatically jump to feeling offended or victimized.

It may not always be about what you did wrong, but you should always be willing to check yourself first.

Prayer: Father, help me know the difference between protecting what You've called me to do and preventing others from doing what You've called them to do. Give me the wisdom to plant boundaries without barbed wire, to stand firm without pushing others down. Show me how to cultivate confidence that's rooted in Your calling, not in comparison. Thank You that Your garden has room for countless blooms—each unique, yet many similar. In Jesus's name, Amen.

growing forward

Tending the Soil

When have you felt threatened by someone doing something similar to what you do? What was your initial reaction?

What's the difference between a healthy boundary and a territorial attitude in your life?

How might God be asking you to make room for others to bloom in areas similar to yours?

Sowing the Seed

The next time you feel threatened by someone's success or similarities to your work, pause and write down three things you admire about them. Then pray a blessing over their efforts. Notice how this shifts your perspective.

Rooting in Truth

But the wisdom that comes from heaven is first of all pure; then peace-loving, considerate, submissive, full of mercy and good fruit, impartial and sincere.
—James 3:17 (NIV)

Branching Out

Philippians 2:3-4, Galatians 6:4-5, Romans 12:18

seeds of thought

seeds of thought

sometimes letting go
isn't surrender—
it's making room
for the field
waiting to find
its abundance in petals
#barefacedjournals

-day eight-
when pretty isn't safe

"Brothers and sisters, I do not consider myself yet to have taken hold of it. But one thing I do: Forgetting what is behind and straining toward what is ahead, I press on toward the goal to win the prize for which God has called me heavenward in Christ Jesus."
—Philippians 3:13-14 (NIV)

I guess the tree that I've loved all these years—the one all my girls took their growing up years' pictures by— the one that made it (although battered up through the ice storm of 2007) is deciding to take itself down. For 18 years, I watched parts of that tree dying off, knowing one day I would have to make a choice, or the choice would be made for me.

Pretty isn't always beneficial. Sometimes you must let go of the things that can inflict harm and know that something is waiting that is better. The tree that frames your daughter's fifth birthday photo is the same one that could crash through your roof during the next Missouri tornado.

I kept telling my hubby I wasn't ready to let it go. But readiness doesn't dictate timing, does it? Not with trees, not with life.

Destruction or disappointment doesn't mean defeat.

When the tornadic winds of Southwest Missouri come rushing through with their tantrums, they don't exactly ask for our permission. They threaten to take out every bit of progress we've made—every good thing we've been trying to do with house renovations. One tree falling the wrong way could undo months of work in seconds.

Even the most courageous gardener knows that yes, you plant, but first there are some things you have to be willing to remove. That half-dying tree still produced the most gorgeous blooms every spring. Even in its brokenness, beauty persisted—but beauty can become a burden when it blinds us to danger.

> *Sometimes letting go isn't surrender—*
> *it's making room for what's next to bloom.*

We weather ice storms and tornadoes—both the literal Missouri kind and the metaphorical ones that tear through the landscapes our hearts. Parts of us may be dying, but other parts still bloom. We hold onto things long past their season simply because they once held beauty. We ignore the warning signs, the slow decay, the potential danger growing with every storm.

Eighteen years is a long time to watch something slowly failing. Eighteen years of knowing but not wanting to know. Eighteen years of beautiful blooms on increasingly fragile branches. The choice I avoided making was eventually made for me when the most prominent branch came crashing down, and quite frankly took out most of the blooms with it.

What's waiting in that newly opened space? What can be grown in that new full sun space?

> *There's mercy in that forced release, in having the*
> *decision taken from our white-knuckled grip. Making*
> *room for the new sometimes means saying goodbye to*
> *what was once beautiful but has become a burden.*

And yes—sometimes we need a better chainsaw for the task. I've already asked for one for Mother's Day.

Prayer: Father God, thank you for your gentle persistence even when I resist necessary change. Help me recognize when I'm clinging to beauty that has become a burden. Give me courage to let go of what's dying so new life can emerge in those spaces. When tornadic winds threaten, teach me to trust your protection more than my own plans. Show me the mercy in forced releases and the grace in decisions taken from my grip. Help me see beyond what was to what could be in newly opened spaces. In Jesus's name, Amen.

growing forward

Tending the Soil
What beautiful thing in your life is turning into a burden or something potentially harm?

Where have you been resisting necessary change because of sentimental attachment?

What "newly opened space" in your life is waiting for God to fill with something new?

Sowing the Seed
Look around your home or yard for something you've kept far past its usefulness simply because of emotional attachment. Consider whether it's time to release it, making space for something new.

Rooting in Truth
"Forgetting what is behind and straining toward what is ahead, I press on toward the goal to win the prize for which God has called me heavenward in Christ Jesus."
—Philippians 3:13-14 (NIV)

Branching Out
Ecclesiastes 3:1-6, Isaiah 43:18-19, 2 Corinthians 5:17

seeds of thought

section two

FLOURISHING IN
NEW SOIL

revived from

the root up

**When challenge helps us blossom into
embracing our most authentic selves, our
greatest transformations
begin in unfamiliar ground.**

to sleep
to regain my balance
as it's useless
to poke around in
the darkness that
holds tired pain in
its remembering.
i don't need to keep
touching my past
to be better for
moving beyond it
#barefacedjournals

-day nine-
when your garden needs to rest

**Forget the former things; do not dwell on the past.
See, I am doing a new thing! Now it springs up;
do you not perceive it? I am making a way in the
wilderness and streams in the wasteland.
— Isaiah 43:18-19 (NIV)**

I like to call it the "season of stuck." You know that place
where you feel like you're going absolutely nowhere?
Your feet might as well be planted in mud. Your dreams
feel buried under layers of everyday responsibilities.
Your purpose seems like it's on pause.

I've been there. I felt this way profoundly when my job
of 16 years as editor of a youth magazine came to a
close. After my mental health break, God gave me a
year to rest, but He didn't inform me that the end of my
break would culminate in going into fundraising. I was
like, "Seriously, God? This is the plan?"

I helped a lot of ministry organizations during that time
and gained new perspective, but it didn't line up with
what I felt God had put on my heart—my purpose, my
degree, my passion.

*I found myself questioning, "Why did you give
me this passion if I can't even operate in it?" I was so
frustrated with the lack of visible progress.*

I remember crying out, "God, give me something. I'll
even do what I do if I have to do it for free!" (Those

are scary words to throw out there, by the way—be prepared if you pray them!)

This concept really hit me when I was watching farmers practice crop rotation. They'll intentionally leave a field unplanted for a season. To anyone driving by, it looks like nothing's happening—just bare dirt.

I wondered, "What if my 'stuck' season is actually God allowing my ground to rest? What if things are still moving underneath, even when I'm frustrated by the lack of growth I can see?"

Think about those farmers. Any good gardener knows that incredible activity is taking place beneath the surface. Microorganisms multiplying. Nutrients rebuilding. The soil becoming richer and more fertile for when it's time to plant again.

The truth is, we often look at being stuck as a negative thing—a state to escape. But what if it's more like a field resting between harvests? What if God is doing essential work in the unseen places of our lives?

We get stuck for all kinds of reasons. Sometimes it's procrastination (I'm so guilty of this—as a writer, the very last thing I do for any magazine issue is write my own article!). Sometimes it's fear of failure. Sometimes it's because we're just plain worn out.

Your ground isn't barren; it's preparing.

What's causing your stuckness right now? Could it be you're so caught in the monotony that you've lost sight of the meaning? We get stuck in our to-do lists—getting up in the morning, cooking, getting everybody out the door, working—and we lose ourselves. We fail to see the connectedness of all we do.

Or maybe, like in that movie "Groundhog Day," you're stuck because you've been focused on yourself rather than how you might serve others.

In the movie, Bill Murray's character is trapped in the same day over and over until he learns to shift his focus from self-serving to serving others. He dedicated himself to learning about people, enriching his mind, learning to play piano, saving lives, and rescuing people. Even in monotony, he found meaning and grew internally.

> *Purpose often emerges when we stop asking "What's in it for me?" and start asking " Who can I bless today?"*

Here's the thing about being stuck: sometimes what looks like a total waste of time is actually just your garden getting ready for something amazing. That project that fizzled out? Those dreams that seemed to go nowhere? The door that closed when you thought it should've swung wide open? They weren't failures—they were your ground resting, getting all the nutrients it needed for what's coming next.

> *So how do we handle these seasons when our garden needs to rest? Start by asking yourself: What might God be doing beneath the surface right now?*

Put yourself in circles with people who understand that resting seasons are part of growth. And most importantly, use this time to nurture the soil of your heart—spend time in prayer, in Scripture, in rest.

Maybe today it's just writing down what's happening beneath your visible surface. What strengths are developing? What character is being built? What dreams are taking deeper root?

Remember, even when gardens appear dormant, there's incredible activity happening underground. Seeds waiting. Roots strengthening. Soil enriching. Everything preparing for the moment when new growth will burst forth.

The signs of life in your resting garden are already forming. Do you see them? That little sprout of possibility? That hint of green pushing through? That's your new season beginning. That's your garden preparing to bloom.

Prayer: Father, help me trust the process when my garden needs to rest. Show me the value in these quieter seasons when visible growth seems halted. Give me eyes to see what You're developing beneath the surface. Teach me to find meaning in the waiting and purpose in the preparation. Like a field being restored between harvests, help me embrace this necessary season of replenishment, knowing You're preparing me for something new. In Jesus's name, Amen.

growing forward

Tending the Soil
What areas of your life feel like they need to rest right now? What might God be restoring beneath the surface?

Are you frustrated by a lack of visible progress? What could be happening in the unseen places of your life?

How might this season of "stuckness" actually be preparation for your next season of growth?

Sowing the Seed
Choose one area where you feel stuck, and write down three possible ways God might be working beneath the surface. Then identify one small, nurturing action you can take this week—not to force growth, but to tend the soil of your heart during this resting season.

Rooting in Truth
Forget the former things; do not dwell on the past. See, I am doing a new thing! Now it springs up; do you not perceive it?" —Isaiah 43:18-19 (NIV)

Branching Out
Ecclesiastes 3:1-4, Psalm 46:10, Hebrews 4:9-11

seeds of thought

seeds of thought

the beauty of green
hides familiar holes
the same old struggles
i fall
i rise
in the move
toward better
determined stems
to find strength in
the desire to grow
with each step forward
however small
#barefacedjournals

-day ten -
luscious grass & hidden pits:

**Therefore, if anyone is in Christ, the new creation
has come: the old has gone, the new is here!
—2 Corinthians 5:17 (NIV)**

Have you ever noticed how we keep tripping over the
same stuff no matter how hard we try to move forward?
That's exactly what happened in my backyard after the
Missouri ice storm of 2007. Our massive 80-foot oak
tree—the one that had stood watching over our family
for decades—came crashing down, and boy, did it leave
a mess behind.

For years afterward, that fallen giant's root system left
these crazy hidden pits all over our yard. The grass,
stubborn and determined as it always is, eventually
grew luscious and green over these holes. Walking
across what looked like a perfectly beautiful lawn
became this weird game of "don't break a leg."

> *No matter how many times I reminded myself
> those pits were lurking under that pretty grass,
> I'd still manage to step in just the wrong spot
> and find myself stumbling. Again. And again.*

Isn't that just like our walk with Jesus?

We grow. We learn. We get more mature in our faith.
Luscious green growth covers our lives, and you can
see God's working on us.

Yet beneath all that spiritual progress, we still find ourselves tripping over the same old stuff—those reactions, patterns, and struggles that we've been dealing with forever.

That beautiful growth in our lives doesn't get rid of the pits; sometimes it even hides them until—boom!—we're face-planting again in the exact same spot we swore we'd avoid.

I've asked myself a million times, "Why do I keep tripping over the same things? Why, after all these years of walking with Jesus, am I still dealing with the same old junk?"

I can see how God's changed me—there's real growth happening. Yet somehow, I still find myself in those "don't break a leg" moments with struggles I thought I'd dealt with ages ago.

The apostle Paul got this when he wrote in Philippians 1:6, "Being confident of this, that he who began a good work in you will carry it on to completion until the day of Christ Jesus" (NIV).

Notice he doesn't say the work is done but keeps going—like how that determined grass keeps growing, keeps reaching, keeps moving toward better even when it hits the same hard spots over and over.

My dad kept these lists—practical stuff like "paint front door" right alongside heart matters like "be a better father" and "be a better husband." I'll never forget when my brother-in-law Rob shared the list at Dad's funeral for the first time, it was like getting this amazing gift from heaven. Even when he kept tripping over the same issues, he never just said, "Well that's just the way I operate." He saw the pits in his own life and truly desired healing.

Like the grass that persistently grows even in tough soil conditions, our growth isn't about never tripping but about getting back up and still wanting to be better.

Can we just be honest and realize the areas of our lives where we keep falling? Can we name those same old pits we keep toppling into instead of pretending they're not there?

Can we stay hungry for the desire for change? Not because we feel ashamed, but because we just know there's something better waiting?

Can we actively do something to move to better? Are we willing to stop ourselves or have others remind us that we are going in that direction. Maybe that action is a code word our people can express when tensions rise, or daily habits that help us see the pits before we fall in. We need to have friends who'll lovingly say, "Hey, watch out, you're about to step in that hole again."

Our struggle with familiar pits doesn't mean we're failing—it just shows we're still in process, still moving toward what God's creating in us.

So, the next time you trip over a familiar challenge, remember my crazy post-storm backyard. No matter how much luscious grass in my yard was obstacles I had to be aware of and navigate again and again— just like our recurring struggles are places when we constantly need God's help to stay upright.

The hidden pits beneath all that luscious grass don't vanish overnight, but with stubborn determination we can get out a shovel to do some filling in, not covering them up, so we get better at not falling in so deep or so often. And until they're filled in, we learn to walk more carefully, holding onto God with everything we've got, moving toward better one small step at a time.

Prayer: Father, thank you for not giving up on me when I keep tripping over the same old stuff. Thank you for being the light I'm reaching for even when I face-plant for the hundredth time. Help me be real about my familiar stumbling spots, stay hungry for change, and do something practical about it. When I fall, remind me you're not rolling your eyes—you're just waiting to help me move toward better. In Jesus's name, Amen.

growing forward

Tending the Soil

What "hidden pits" do you keep tripping over in your life, despite the beautiful growth around them?

When you face-plant over the same old struggles, what's your typical response?

Like the grass that stubbornly grows over difficult terrain, where have you seen persistent growth in your life despite challenging circumstances?

Sowing the Seed

Take a moment to identify your most persistent "hidden pit"—that struggle you keep falling into despite your best efforts. Write down one practical strategy (like a code word with a trusted friend or a new daily habit) to navigate around this pit. Consider sharing your strategy with someone who will lovingly alert you when your veering in the wrong direction.

Rooting in Truth

Therefore, if anyone is in Christ, the new creation has come: The old has gone, the new is here!
—2 Corinthians 5:17 (NIV)

Branching Out

Philippians 1:6, Romans 7:15-25, Galatians 6:9

seeds of thought

seeds of thought

withered stems droop downward
shortening each anxious breath
it's in the pruning of dead things
that peace finds room to rest
no memory stays perfect
when clutched in fearful hands
only what's freed finds purpose
in God's unfolding plans
#barefacedjournals

-day eleven-

pruning season

**"Forgetting what is behind and straining toward
what is ahead, I press on..."**
—Philippians 3:13-14 (NIV)

Have you ever watched a skilled gardener prune? It can
seem almost brutal—cutting away branches that look
perfectly fine to the untrained eye.

*But that gardener knows the secret to flourishing
foliage: growth requires cutting away the dead stuff.*

I've been in this place lately, fixating on goals left
unfinished, problems still unresolved, and regrets that
just won't seem to pack their bags and leave. It's way
easier to dwell on the "if onlys..." than to celebrate how
far I've come.

There's something about life's transitions that makes us
nostalgic, isn't there? We look back with that bittersweet
feeling—like pressing flowers between pages to
preserve them while knowing they'll never be quite the
same as when they were alive and vibrant in the garden.

*The most beautiful gardens require regular,
intentional pruning—and so do our hearts and finds.*

I've noticed we tend to mentally box up bright moments
as "gone forever" while dragging painful regrets around
like dead branches, wondering why we feel so weighed

down. We become spiritual hoarders, unwilling to snip away what no longer serves God's purpose in our lives.

But Paul gives us the best approach for moving forward: "Forgetting what is behind and straining toward what is ahead. I PRESS ON..." He understood that spiritual pruning shears are essential tools for the journey.

Some seasons in our lives need to be composted, broken down into nourishment instead of being stored up as an unyielding memory to regret that does not serve us.

As C.S. Lewis wrote, "There are far, far better things ahead than any we leave behind." The comfort of Christ can overcome regret's relentless root system if we practice intentionally cutting it back and releasing it into His care.

James 1:17 reminds us, "Every good gift is from above." As you tend your inner garden, may you have the courage to prune away what no longer serves, recall the good gifts that helped you grow, and leave any heavy stones behind so you can enter your next season with open hands to receive fresh blooms and blessings in the days ahead.

Prayer: Lord of all seasons, sometimes I hang onto dead things way too long—regrets, disappointments, failures that you've already forgiven. Help me learn the gentle art of pruning, of knowing when to let go so new life can emerge. Give me the courage to compost my regrets into your care, and open hands to receive the good gifts you've got waiting in this next season. In Jesus's name, Amen.

growing forward

Tending the Soil
What area of your life might God be pruning right now?

What "dead branches" of regret or past failures are you still carrying?

How have previous seasons of pruning ultimately led to greater fruitfulness?

Sowing the Seed
Choose one regret that you need to release. Write it down, pray over it, then physically destroy the paper (tear it up, burn it safely, etc.) as a symbol of letting it go.

Rooting in Truth
"Forgetting what is behind and straining toward what is ahead, I press on..." —Philippians 3:13-14 (NIV)

Branching Out
John 15:1-5, Hebrews 12:1-3, 2 Corinthians 5:17

seeds of thought

seeds of thought

celebrate one bud
finding its bloom
on the greenest bush
because green is
just the transformation
of the flower to find
a steady footing
to hold its petals
#barefacedjournals

-day twelve-
unnoticed elegance

**Consider how the wild flowers grow. They do not
labor or spin. Yet I tell you, not even Solomon in all
His splendor was dressed like one of these.**
—Luke 12:27 (NIV)

I've always been drawn to the quiet perfection of plants
that thrive without an audience.

When I first moved into my house, something magical
caught my eye—tiny white flowers cradling miniature
strawberries growing randomly throughout my lawn.

No garden beds, no caretaker, just these pristine little
berries putting on a spectacular show for absolutely
no one. I marveled at how long they must have been
blooming there, season after season, with countless
people driving past without ever noticing their minute,
elegant display.

These wild strawberries appear for only about a month
each year. What fascinated me most was that even the
birds seemed to overlook this mini berry feast. Nature's
perfect design, completely unappreciated.

Sometimes I've questioned, "If no one notices my work,
my effort, my beauty—does what I do honestly matter?"

*In our world of metrics, likes, and visibility, we've
absorbed the lie that unnoticed elegance lacks value.*

Look, I'll be honest—I struggle with this too. I love when people notice my work, and I'm not above checking how many likes my posts get.

It's so human to want that validation, right?

But those miniature berries didn't need my validation to fulfill their purpose. They existed simply because that's what they were created to do—to bring unexpected beauty into an ordinary lawn, whether anyone appreciated them or not.

God's view on value operates differently from ours.

Jesus pointed to wildflowers—not cultivated garden blooms, but common field flowers—and declared their unnoticed splendor greater than Solomon's royal attire. No human labored over them or photographed them for social media, yet their beauty fulfilled a divine purpose.

In Matthew 6:4, Jesus tells us our Father "sees what is done in secret," suggesting there's something sacred about goodness that doesn't demand attention—excellence without audience, beauty without applause.

When the magazine I worked for closed and I found myself in fundraising, I created my own publication called *Paint & Puddles.*

I wasn't seeking wide circulation; I simply needed to express the gift within me. In fact, my audience was just me and Father.

I find such comfort in this truth. When I feel unseen or unnoticed, I remember those strawberries thriving without applause. I think about my daughters' art projects when they were little—pictures lovingly created and then stuffed in a drawer. The joy wasn't in someone else seeing their creation; it was in the creating itself. Isn't that how God designed us too?

Those wild strawberries taught me that what goes unnoticed often grows us the most. The flowers within us don't need spotlights to fulfill their purpose—just nurturing attention. Their value isn't diminished by invisibility.

Today, I challenge myself (and you) to find joy in unnoticed elegance. To pour love and excellence into life's forgotten corners.

To bloom brilliantly even when no human acknowledges your display. Our Father, who sees in secret, delights in the beauty we bring to this world— whether witnessed by thousands or existing as a sacred secret between just Him and us.

Prayer: Father, forgive me for the times I've measured my worth by visibility and affirmation. Help me find joy in unnoticed elegance—in bringing beauty to places where it might never be acknowledged by human eyes. Remind me that You see what is done in secret, and that's enough. Give me the courage to bloom brilliantly even in forgotten corners, knowing that fulfilling Your purpose for my life doesn't require human applause. In Jesus's name, Amen.

growing forward

Tending the Soil
What beautiful things do you do that often go unnoticed or unappreciated?

How does your motivation change when you know your efforts won't be publicly recognized?

Where might God be inviting you to create beauty or pursue excellence that only He might see?

Sowing the Seed
This week, do something beautiful that no one else will see—plant flowers in an overlooked spot, write an encouraging note to someone who won't know it was you, or create something lovely just for the joy of creating. Pay attention to how it feels when you're creating without the promise of recognition—that's where you might find the purest joy.

Rooting in Truth
"Consider how the wild flowers grow. They do not labor or spin. Yet I tell you, not even Solomon in all His splendor was dressed like one of these." —Luke 12:27 (NIV)

Branching Out
Matthew 6:1-4, Colossians 3:23-24, Psalm 139:13-16

seeds of thought

i will not allow doubt
to overwrite my
confidence in the
goodness i know
God is working out
in the step-by-step
day-by-day
if i'd but open
my eyes to see
the abundance
surrounding my feet
#barefacedjournals

-day thirteen-
flowering assurance

And why do you worry about clothes? See how the flowers of the field grow. They do not labor or spin. Yet I tell you that not even Solomon in all His splendor was dressed like one of these.
—Matthew 6:28-29 (NIV)

You know what's crazy? I can spend an entire morning stressing about bills, deadlines, and all the what ifs that crowd my brain. Meanwhile, I'm driving right past hundreds of wildflowers that haven't spent a single second worrying about anything.

I noticed this one day when I was stuck in traffic, mind spinning with my to-do list that seemed to multiply faster than I could check things off. My stomach was in knots over a deadline, and I was mentally calculating if I had enough money to cover an unexpected car repair AND pay the utility bill.

That's when I spotted them—these bright purple wildflowers growing in the median. Right there between lanes of speeding cars, exhaust fumes, and zero attention, these little blooms were putting on a show like they had nothing better to do than just be gorgeous.

Nobody planted them. Nobody watered them.
Nobody fertilized them or protected them
from being trampled.

But there they were, doing their wildflower thing without a care in the world. I found myself drawn to their quiet confidence. These flowers weren't worried about their circumstances—they were simply thriving where they'd been placed, receiving what God provided and turning it into beauty.

And then it hit me what Jesus was talking about with the lilies. He wasn't just giving a cute nature lesson. He was calling out our ridiculous tendency to spend our lives freaking out about provision while we're surrounded by evidence that God's got this.

Sure, the not freaking out part is easier said than done when you're eating ramen noodles for a week, just trying to get to the next paycheck before you need to fill up the gas tank.

Believe me, I still have those moments! The funny thing is, I shared this verse with my girls a lot. I've explained how God cares for the flowers, all while my mind was racing with my own financial stresses. Talk about preaching what you need to practice!

It took constantly remembering those flowers to make me realize I needed to reconnect with the words that were coming out of my mouth. And honestly, how many times do we all have to do that?

Flowers don't have savings accounts or insurance policies (not that you shouldn't). They don't worry about blooming "well enough" compared to the flowers down the road. They just receive what God gives each day and turn it into something beautiful. Meanwhile, I'm over here trying to control everything ten steps ahead, as if God's provision depends on my ability to have a plan in place for every eventuality.

The crazy part? Jesus says I'm way more valuable to God than these flowers. If God puts that much care into something that's here today and gone tomorrow, how much more is He looking out for me?

Don't get me wrong—I'm not saying we should ditch responsibility and just "flower power" our way through life. Bills still need paying. Work still needs doing.

> *But there's a massive difference between responsible action and anxiety-fueled panic.*

One moves forward with purpose; the other just spins in circles wearing us out.

I've started using those wildflowers as a kind of reality check. When I feel the familiar tightness of worry creeping in, I look for the nearest bloom or leafy tree and I remind myself: "If God's taking care of this little sprig, He's got everything I need covered—and even more so." Then I shift my focus from the problem to looking for how God is already showing up in the situation.

It's not some magic formula that instantly dissolves all my concerns. But it does help me breathe again. It helps me remember who's really in charge. Thank goodness it is not me. And it helps me focus on watching for God's hand at work instead of fixating on what might go wrong.

So next time you're spiraling into worry mode, try it. Find a flower—any flower—and really look at it. Notice how it's not freaking out about anything. Notice how it's fully provided for without a single worry. And then remember that the God who designed that intricate little bloom knows exactly what you need too.

> *Ask yourself: "Have I seen what God has done before? He'll do it again." Then start looking for Him to show up.*

Lovelies, maybe we'd all be a little better off if we spent less time spinning our wheels and more time considering the lilies.

Prayer: God, I'll be honest—sometimes I overcomplicate things when You've made the path so clear. Thank You for constantly reminding me: "Have you seen what I've done? I'll do it again." When I start spinning into stress mode, help me take a breath, and watch for how You're already working. I want to trust You like those flowers do—with complete confidence that the One who made me has already made a way for me. Teach me to find rest in Your faithful provision. In Jesus's name, Amen.

growing forward

Tending the Soil
1. What are you currently worrying about that you could entrust to God?

2. How has God proven His faithfulness to you in the past?

3. Where do you see evidence of God's provision in the world around you today?

Sowing the Seed
The next time anxiety begins to rise, find the nearest plant or flower. Study it briefly and pray, "Lord, if you care for this [plant/flower], how much more do you care for me?"

Rooting in Truth
And why do you worry about clothes? See how the flowers of the field grow. They do not labor or spin.
—Matthew 6:28 (NIV)

Branching Out
Philippians 4:6-7, 1 Peter 5:7, Luke 12:22-31

seeds of thought

seeds of thought

i have yet to find
good reason to live
beyond the sensibility
of flowers that
flourish without
the need for
flattery
#barefacedjournals

-day fourteen-
blooming beyond the labels

**That means we will not compare ourselves
with each other as if one of us were better or another
worse. We have far more interesting things to do
with our lives. Each of us is an original.**
— Galatians 5:26 (MSG)

Have you ever walked through a botanical garden
and looked at those little plant identification stakes?
"Monkey Face Orchid," "Butter Butt Coneflower,"
"Dead Man's Fingers," "Lobster Claw Plant," "Skunk
Cabbage." Those are actual plant names that make me
laugh and wonder—who in the world comes up with
these? Some botanist from centuries ago just decided
"I'm going to call you this," slapped on a label, and now
everyone accepts it as fact. But the flowers themselves?
They just keep blooming, completely unaware of the
ridiculous names we've given them.

Just like those plants in the garden, we humans spend
our lives being labeled too—by others, by society,
sometimes even by ourselves. "The shy one." "The
failure." "The addict." "The divorced." These labels
can stick with us for years—defining us by our worst
moments, our struggles, or just one small aspect of
who we are. And unlike flowers, we actually hear these
labels, internalize them, and let them shape what we
believe is possible for our lives.

The Bible is full of people who could have been
confined by their labels. Consider Rahab—a woman

whose story powerfully illustrates how limiting our labels can be.

There's a pin floating around social media that says: "Joshua 2: Rahab, the Prostitute" and right beneath it, "Matthew 1: Rahab, the grandmother of the Messiah."

But I'm as guilty as anyone of always thinking of her as "Rahab the prostitute" rather than "Rahab, great-great-grandma of Jesus." Isn't that crazy? This woman's entire identity has been reduced to what she did before she even met God, rather than the incredible legacy she became part of in the lineage of Christ.

Why is it that the derogatory label sticks so much more firmly than the honorable one?

One sin—one season of her life—has become her permanent identity marker for thousands of years. Someone just decided to stick that label in her soil, and we've all been reading it ever since.

I know dealing with a mental health label is challenging. I don't like saying I have experienced psychotic episodes—it's not exactly something you lead with at a dinner party! Very few people would associate that with the person they see editing a Christian women's magazine or writing books. I had to struggle with the cone of shame of that label for a long time. But I've learned something important: labels might identify a part of my growth process, but they don't define the full bloom of who I am.

Think about it: we live in this greenhouse culture where everyone thinks they can peer in and identify exactly what type of plant we are.

"There goes Juliet, the 'Scaredy Cat Plant,'" or "Watch out for Todd, he's definitely a 'Prickly Pear.'" They watch us on social media and make snap judgments. Let's be honest—we don't show people everything. I mean, if I really sat in my reality here, I would literally be sitting in a load of laundry piled miles high, because I'm a messy person. I admit it! And yet we're letting strangers stick plant markers in our soil based on the tiniest fraction of knowledge about our lives.

> *But SURPRISE! The plant stakes people try to place beside us don't have to determine what we'll grow into.*

Maybe you've been labeled "Weeping Willow" because of past mistakes. Maybe you're carrying around a diagnosis that makes you feel like a "Bleeding Heart." Maybe it's anxiety, addiction recovery, divorce, or some other word that seems to overshadow every beautiful petal about you.

We make these comparisons constantly. Upward comparisons with those we think are "Shooting Stars" versus us, and downward comparisons with those we believe are "Wallflowers." And in all that comparing, we're letting labels define not just others, but ourselves.

In my book, "Leading Ladies: Discover Your God-Grown Strategy for Success," my co-author Lisa Burris Burns and I shared the story of award-winning music artist Katie Nicole about her crushing anxiety—the kind that stops you in your tracks, completely immobilizing you. But it was in those exact moments of anxiety that God used her to write some of the most profound worship lyrics the church has seen in years.

> *What if she had let her "Sensitive Plant" label determine her limitations? What if she had believed that her anxiety disqualified her from flowering in ministry?*

I wonder how many people she helps when she stands on stage and says, "I have life-controlling, crushing anxiety, but God has given me the power to be here." That's what happens when we refuse to let the plant stakes others place beside us control what kind of bloom we'll become.

> *You are not what people call you. You're not a "Sausage Tree" or a "Strangler Fig." You are what God created you to be.*

Jesus himself was labeled. The religious types of His day saw Him as a thorn who was always pushing over tables as recorded in Matthew 21:12. But His closest friends—those who spent time with Him daily—knew Him differently.

> *Even Jesus didn't reveal His full identity to everyone. In fact He was selective about the people who He confirmed His true identity with.*

He revealed himself through His actions and teachings, allowing those around him to discover His true nature in their own time.

When God created man and woman, He looked at His creation and called them "good." Not "Stinking Corpse Lily." Not "Devil's Claw." Not "Too Flashy Bird of Paradise" or "Plain Jane Greens." Just good. God is the Master Gardener who planted us, designed us, breathed life into us. From the beginning, He equipped you with exactly the right characteristics to thrive in the environment He placed you in.

> *So often, the labels life kicks our way diminish what we think and feel about all that potential God planted in us.*

Sometimes labels cover up our true colors entirely. We don't even know they're there. It takes a true miracle for

Him to unearth it all and say, "See, this beautiful bloom has been here all along."

Galatians 5:26 reminds us: "We will not compare ourselves with each other as if one of us were better or another worse. We have far more interesting things to do with our lives. Each of us is an original."

> *You know what? It's time for us to pull up some of these plant stakes we've been living with and refuse to let others stick them in our heads again.*

It's time to remember that someone just made up these labels and decided they fit us. But ultimately, it should be God's choice, as our Creator and Master Gardener, to determine what we'll become. And I know He has some even more beautiful blooms He's growing in you.

Prayer: Father, forgive me for accepting labels that don't come from You. Help me see myself through Your eyes— as an original creation designed to bloom in unique ways. When others try to define me with their strange plant stakes and identification tags, give me the courage to hold fast to Your truth instead. Show me how to speak life-giving words over others, pulling up the confining markers they've been given. Thank You that my identity is secure in You, not in the ever-changing opinions of those around me. In Jesus's name, Amen.

growing forward

Tending the Soil
1. What labels have you allowed to define you that don't align with God's view of you?

2. In what areas of your life do you find yourself comparing yourself to others?

3. What unique qualities has God planted in you that the world might try to minimize?

Sowing the Seed
Take a moment to write down three labels you've carried that don't reflect your true identity. Beside each one, write the truth God says about you. Choose one of these truths to speak over yourself daily this week

Rooting in Truth
"We will not compare ourselves with each other as if one of us were better or another worse. We have far more interesting things to do with our lives. Each of us is an original." — Galatians 5:26 (MSG)

Branching Out
1 Samuel 16:7, Ephesians 2:10, Psalm 139:13-14

seeds of thought

out of the thousands
you picked me
your words gently
roll down my petals
pulling drops from my eyes
wrapped in the heat
of your hand
your loving gaze secures me
in the snug of deep-pockets
to pull this wilty flower
out in proud display
#barefacedjournals

-day fifteen-
his wilty flower

**Come to me, all you who are weary
and burdened, and I will give you rest.
— Matthew 11:28 (NIV)**

Have you ever watched a child pick a wildflower? The
way they tuck it carefully into a pocket or hold it gently
in their small hand? There's something beautiful
about how they treasure that simple bloom—not for its
perfection, but simply because they chose it.

They don't discard it when it begins to wilt. Instead, that
drooping flower becomes even more precious because
it reminds them of the joy they felt when they first
discovered it.

I wonder if that's how God sees us—not as perfect,
perpetually blooming specimens, but as beloved
treasures He keeps close to His heart in every season
of our growth. We live in a culture that worships
productivity. We're constantly measuring our worth by
what we can produce, achieve, or contribute.

*Even in our spiritual lives, we can fall into the
trap of thinking we need to be constantly blooming—
always vibrant, always fruitful, always "on" for God.
We burden ourselves with an exhausting spiritual
performance that Jesus never asked for.*

I'm reminded of Mary and Martha, those sisters who
loved Jesus in such different ways. When Jesus came to
visit, Martha rushed around preparing everything, while

Mary simply sat at His feet. When Martha complained, Jesus gently reminded her: "Martha, Martha, you are worried and upset about many things, but few things are needed—or indeed only one. Mary has chosen what is better, and it will not be taken away from her." (Luke 10:38-42, NIV)

What was that "one thing" Mary chose? Simply being present with Jesus.

Many of us are stuck in Martha-mode, thinking our spiritual value comes from what we do for God rather than who we are to Him. We've convinced ourselves that unless we're blooming spectacularly, we're somehow failing Him.

But what if our seasons of quiet, of rest, of simply being with Him are actually the moments he treasures most?

I remember a powerful experience during worship where God opened my eyes to see myself as a carefree child playing with Jesus. We splashed in clear water, made mud pies, and picked fruit together. Animals gathered around us—a lamb, chipmunks, a gentle fawn. In that moment, I sensed God whispering, "This is what I want from you—your presence, your companionship. You don't have to strive or perform to earn my love."

I wept as I realized that even though I was doing everything to show Jesus how much I loved Him, he didn't require it.

He was showing me the thick wrap of His love that was my constant—the only thing He wanted me to do was enjoy the gift of His never-changing love for me.

It reminds me of Psalm 34:8: "Taste and see that the Lord is good." God didn't say "Think about my goodness" or "Let's have a theological debate about whether I'm good." He said TASTE it—experience it!

Enjoy it! It's like taking a bite of a perfectly ripe pear—God wants us to take time to enjoy His goodness, he wants to lavish on us, that has nothing to do with what we can do to earn His good things.

Even when I'm not at my brightest or best, when my petals are drooping and I'm feeling far from vibrant, He still treasures me and keeps me near. He doesn't wait until I'm doing the right things to cherish me.

He loves me in my wilty moments, my tired seasons, and my not-quite-there-yet phases. If I lean right up against His heart I can hear its steady beat reminding me I'm His.

In Matthew 11:28, Jesus invites us: "Come to me, all you who are weary and burdened, and I will give you rest." Notice He doesn't say, "Come to me when you're at your best" or "Come to me when you've got it all together." He specifically invites us in our weariness, in our burdened state—in our wilting moments.

We're drawn to His presence because he's placed that desire in our hearts. God plants goodness in our path everywhere—from the simplest wildflower nodding in the breeze to jaw-dropping miracles that can't be explained any other way. He's constantly scattering evidence of His love around us.

In a world that constantly demands more—more productivity, more perfection, more performance—this truth remains: Everything he wants is you.

Not what you can do, not what you can achieve, not what you can become someday. Just you, today, as you are, resting in His presence like a flower tucked in His pocket, near to His heart and in the center of His mind.

Prayer: Father, thank you for cherishing me in every season—not just when I'm beautifully blooming, but also in my wilting moments. Help me release the need to perform for Your love and instead rest in the knowledge that You keep me close to Your heart exactly as I am. Teach me to receive Your never-changing love and to recognize the goodness You have planted all along my path. In Jesus's name, Amen.

growing forward

Tending the Soil
When do you find yourself slipping into "Martha mode," believing your worth comes from what you do rather than who you are to God?

What are some "love notes from God" you've noticed in your life recently—those everyday blessings that remind you of His care?

How might your relationship with God change if you truly believed He cherishes you even in your "wilty" seasons?

Sowing the Seed
Take a moment to simply be still in God's presence this week. Set a timer for 5 minutes and just sit with Him, not asking for anything or trying to accomplish anything spiritual. Simply receive His love and cherishing presence.

Rooting in Truth
"Come to me, all you who are weary and burdened, and I will give you rest." — Matthew 11:28 (NIV)

Branching Out
Psalm 34:8, Luke 10:38-42, Isaiah 30:15

seeds of thought

seeds of thought

just want one lifetime of answers

just want one drop in the pool

just want one minute of dreaming

and all the faith to come through

to see clouds from the upside of down

to let sun press grey skies blue

one bud to push the rocky deeps

to hold one moment of air

to root a stoney persistence

and all the strength of my knees

so that the smallness of seedling

may find the bigness of trees

#barefacedjournals

-day fifteen -
regret-me-knots

**"Be kind to one another, tenderhearted, forgiving
one another, as God in Christ forgave you."
—Ephesians 4:32 (ESV)**

Have you ever noticed how certain plants can take over
a garden? I was looking at our lawn this week and saw
these small flowers spreading everywhere, reminding
me of forget-me-nots in how quickly they multiply. Left
unchecked, they spread rapidly, claiming territory that
wasn't meant for them. It got me thinking about how
similar things can happen in our hearts.

I call these emotional weeds our "regret-me-knots" –
those embarrassing moments, painful failures, and
cringe-worthy mistakes that keep blooming in our
minds, demanding that we never forget them.

*Similarly, the seeds of offense find fertile soil
in our hearts whenever we stew in hurt feelings
instead of extending grace.*

It feels like everybody is just looking for something
to get upset about these days. Whether it's political
disagreements, theological differences, or personal
slights, many people seem ready to blow up at any
second. Our social media feeds become perfectly tilled
soil for cultivating gardens of resentment rather than
compassion.

Jesus knew this tendency well. He warned us, "A person's enemies will be those of his own household" (Matthew 10:36 ESV).

The question isn't whether conflicts will come—they will—but how we respond when they do.

Will we let the weeds of offense spread unchecked through our emotional gardens? Or will we practice the discipline of regular weeding—forgiving quickly, releasing hurts, and making space for beautiful growth?

When Jesus was arrested and facing false accusations, "he did not retaliate; when he suffered, he made no threats" (1 Peter 2:23 NIV). He stood calmly because he fully trusted God's bigger plan. He knew some plants need pruning for greater fruitfulness later.

Similarly, Paul understood the importance of intentional gardening in our thought lives: "Forgetting what lies behind and straining forward to what lies ahead" (Philippians 3:13 ESV). When we allow regrets and offenses to root deeply, they drain the soil of nutrients meant for fruits of the Spirit: love, joy, peace, patience, kindness, goodness, faithfulness, gentleness, and self-control.

Here's the thing about spiritual gardening: you get to choose what you cultivate. You can either keep watering offenses and regrets, or you can nurture forgiveness and growth.

Instead of letting these emotional weeds spread unchecked, we can transform them into growth opportunities. Even better, we can plant something beautiful in the very soil where our regrets and offenses once grew. That painful experience? It's now growing compassion you never had before. That huge mistake? It's fertilizing wisdom that no success ever could.

God wants us to cultivate a different kind of garden in our minds and hearts. He gives us a planting guide in Philippians 4:8: "Finally, brothers, whatever is true, whatever is honorable, whatever is just, whatever is pure, whatever is lovely, whatever is commendable, if there is any excellence, if there is anything worthy of praise, think about these things" (ESV).

When tensions flare up, as they will, let's be confident enough in God to let Him lead our responses, rather than reactively flinging emotional weedkiller everywhere.

With Him, we can inspire peace, love and unity, even when we're not feeling it. Remember, "the battle is not yours, but God's" (2 Chronicles 20:15 ESV).

Today, what regrets or offenses do you need to stop watering? What old wounds are you allowing to define your landscape?

In Christ, we're a new creation—our garden gets a fresh start. The old plants are cleared away; God's planting something new. Our painful moments aren't the end of our garden—they're just the soil from which God grows something beautiful in our lives.

Prayer: Father, thank You for continually working in the soil of my heart. Forgive me for nurturing offenses and regrets that choke out the fruit You want to grow in me. Help me pull up these emotional weeds by the roots and replace them with forgiveness, grace, and hope. Plant in me a spirit that is quick to forgive and slow to take offense. May the garden of my heart reflect Your beauty rather than my brokenness. In Jesus's name, Amen.

growing forward

Tending the Soil
Identify your regret-me-knots: What past mistakes
or offenses are you allowing to define your emotional
landscape? Take time to identify specific regrets or
offenses you've been nurturing.

Practice intentional forgiveness: Choose one
person this week (including yourself) who needs your
forgiveness. Write a letter expressing your forgiveness
that you may or may not send, but use it as an exercise
to release the offense.

Replace negative thoughts: When a regret surfaces,
immediately counter it with a truth from Scripture.
You can create Scripture cards to help with this
practice.

Plant new growth: Identify one way you can use a
past mistake as fertilizer for new wisdom. How has
God redeemed something difficult in your life to create
beauty?

Rooting in Truth:
"Be kind to one another, tenderhearted, forgiving one
another, as God in Christ forgave you." —Ephesians
4:32 (ESV)

Branching Out
Philippians 3:13-14, Philippians 4:8, 2 Corinthians 5:17

seeds of thought

seeds of thought

let the breeze take its toll
on my leaves
pushing the bend
to my branches
let me find
the sway of the dance
and delight in the
cool slap of the rain
the roll off my hard skins
let the refresh burrow
into the lush of my core
to hold the grounding
of deep rooted strength
let me stand tall
build the platform for the birds
as they push their babies
to find first flight
let me be the safety
to keep the predators at bay
and the dependable shade
#barefacedjournals

-day sixteen-
planted by the water

But blessed is the one who trusts in the Lord, whose confidence is in Him. They will be like a tree planted by the water that sends out its roots by the stream. It does not fear when heat comes; its leaves are always green. It has no worries in a year of drought and never fails to bear fruit.—Jeremiah 17:7-8 (NIV)

Ever felt that bone-deep tired? Not the kind sleep fixes, but the kind that makes you wonder how to take another step forward? When life feels too heavy and the ground keeps shifting beneath you—that's not just physical exhaustion. That's soul tired.

> *Some days I'm drained not because I stopped believing, but because holding onto faith in the chaos is just...a lot.*

I don't want to be disappointed if things don't work out my way, in my timing. I know the truth, but I need to write it down. Need to come back and read it again—not from doubt, but to reconnect with what matters.

I love how Jeremiah 17:7-8 wraps around me. This picture of a tree with roots reaching deep into water. A tree that doesn't panic when rain doesn't come. Why? Its nourishment doesn't depend on what's happening above ground. The stream keeps feeding its roots, no matter what.

Have you seen trees along riverbanks? They lean toward the water, like they know exactly where life comes from.

These trees thrive in harsh places not because they're stronger, but because they've positioned themselves near what gives life.

> *The tree isn't exceptional—*
> *it's exceptionally well-connected.*

This is what we need. To be planted in the right place. To sink our roots into Living Water so when life gets hard—and it will—we don't wither. Instead, we become shade for the weary. Our strength isn't our own—it flows from the One who never runs dry.

But being planted is a choice. We choose where to set our roots, what to draw from. The world offers many temporary wells—success, relationships, validation, distraction—but they dry up. Only God's presence never stops flowing.

I've tried chasing validation through achievement, comfort through relationships, peace through control. Even if it's well-intended it just leads to weariness.

When the world presses in, now I ask myself: where am I planted? Am I reaching for things that won't last, or am I sending my roots deeper into what always sustains?

> *The strongest faith isn't the one that never faces*
> *drought—it's the one that knows where to find water*
> *when everything else has dried up.*

Maybe you're in drought right now. Heat pressing in. That unexpected diagnosis. The relationship hanging by a thread. Bills keeping you up at night. Prayers that seem to bounce back.

When you're rooted in Him, even your driest moments won't consume you. When you're weak, your source is strong. When you have nothing left to give, you'll still bear fruit, because He sustains you.

I've seen this lived out in the most broken places. Friends walking through unimaginable loss with peace that makes no sense. Families navigating devastation with steady hope. Not because they don't hurt—they absolutely do—but because their roots go deeper than their pain.

There's something beautiful about a tree that's weathered storms. Its branches might be scarred, but its trunk stands stronger. Its leaves still provide shade. Its fruit still feeds. Sometimes, the trees that have endured the most become landmarks—guiding others toward the water that saved them.

*The trees that weather storms become beacons—
living proof that what we're rooted in
matters more than what we face.*

Let's be trees by the water, not just for ourselves, but for others. Places of shade and rest for the weary. When heat comes—and it will—we won't fear, because we're planted in Him.

In a world obsessed with quick fixes, let's push our roots deeper into His steady presence.

*There's a difference between hoping circumstances
improve and the hope we have in Jesus. We
draw from someone unchanging. His care ALWAYS
transcends circumstances.*

This passage doesn't just promise survival—it promises thriving. Not just enduring—but bearing fruit. Even when it seems impossible. Especially then.

So sink your roots deep. Press into His presence. Draw from His Word. And watch as he transforms even your emptiest seasons into stories of His faithfulness.

Prayer: Father, I come to you weary and in need of your strength. The world feels overwhelming sometimes, but I don't want to be shaken by what I see. Plant me by your water, Lord. Let my roots grow deep in you, so that I may not wither in the heat of hardship. Help me position myself so that I can continuously draw from your presence. Make me a place of refuge for others—a reminder of your constant provision. Thank you for being my source—the Living Water that never runs dry. When doubt creeps in, remind me of where my strength comes from. When fear rises, anchor me in your unfailing love. I want to be so deeply connected to you that others see your faithfulness in my life. In Jesus's name, Amen.

growing forward

Tending the Soil
1. Where are your roots currently drawing nourishment from? Are these sources life-giving or depleting?

2. When have you experienced God's sustaining presence during a "drought" season?

3. How might your struggles become a testimony that guides others to the Living Water?

Sowing the Seed
Find a picture or plant that represents deep roots. Place it somewhere visible to remind yourself to continually draw from God's presence rather than temporary sources of strength.

Rooting in Truth
"But blessed is the one who trusts in the Lord, whose confidence is in him." —Jeremiah 17:7 (NIV)

Branching Out
Psalm 1:1-3, John 7:37-38, Isaiah 58:11

seeds of thought

seeds of thought

section three

SHINING
RESILIENT HOPE

soak up
the sun

When life struggles feel overwhelming and God seems distant, His light continues to nurture and sustain us through the most challenging seasons.

you are the freshness
of new rain
and the prism of sun
in elegant display
your favor circles my head
to delight my heart
in pouring you out
#barefacedjournals

-day seventeen-
soul wounds to beautiful blooms

**He heals the brokenhearted and binds
up their wounds. —Psalm 147:3 (NIV)**

I love Gerber daisies, but I hate getting them for special
occasions, and my family knows it. Now and then I just
look at them in the cooler at Walmart, thinking about
which bouquet I would pick—their bold colors just
radiate joy. But we all know what happens next, don't
we? A few days later, those perfect daisies began to sag.
And I do what I always do—started plucking them out
one by one as they drooped, tossing away what was no
longer "perfect." Soon all I had left was a sad bunch of
baby's breath and greenery to chuck in the trash.

I remember one Mother's Day, staring at a mangled
bouquet– getting ready to chuck it–vase and all–God
stopped me with a thought that cut straight to my heart:

*'This is how you've been treating your wounded places—
saving face by plucking them out of your perfect bouquet
sight because you think you should be 'over them by now.'*

The truth is, sometimes I've gotten so focused on
everything that I wanted to throw the good and the
bad out in the trash. Have you ever thought, "Maybe I
wouldn't struggle so much if I haven't been damaged by
A, B or C?" Do you ever feel like all the spoiled part of
your story negates all the beauty sometimes. What good
is this to anyone? That's exactly how I've approached
my soul wounds too. I would hide the flowers in the

trash because I didn't want anyone to realize I had thrown their gift away. I just wanted them to disappear and no one know. Just like my pain—buried deep where no one could see it.

In that moment, God used those fading flowers to show me something profound about my spiritual journey. I had been moving through life with soul wounds that I simply refused to acknowledge. I was hiding my pain, determined to appear whole when inside I was withering.

This wasn't just a flower metaphor—it was my lived reality. For years, I concealed unhealed trauma and toxic patterns that I'd allowed into my marriage. When I finally had my mental health breakdown that led me to the psych ward, it all spewed to the surface like a broken septic system.

I was terrified that if people in Christian leadership knew my full story, I would lose my place at the table. My ministry. My voice. My belonging.

My beautiful friend Tracy Glass shared a question that a lady in her church had asked her: "What is holding you back from sharing your complete testimony? Are you afraid of shining too bright, or are you dealing with the shame?"

Those words pierced straight through me. I had spent so long hiding my deepest wounds, even from my family, because that's what I learned growing up as a church girl.

Shut up, put on the face, and show up for service on Sunday morning. I became well-schooled in the art of hiding my pain behind the Bible. After all, if you have Jesus in your life you should be "happy all the day."

However, I didn't realize, the very things I was

ashamed of about people knowing about the real me, were actually evidence of His healing power.

My mama used to tell me, "God didn't bring you through so much to have you keep quiet about it." But vulnerability has a price tag, doesn't it? When we share our authentic struggles, not everyone responds with grace.

Sometimes the very people we hope will understand are the ones who back away, uncomfortable with our messy reality.

God doesn't just repair our broken places; He transforms them into something new and beautiful. Where we once saw only damage and decay, He creates vibrant new life. Our wounds become the very soil where the most stunning blooms can grow—if we'll stop plucking them away and allow Him access to those tender places.

How many of us are still moving through life pretending everything's fine? We're afraid that if we acknowledge our pain, we'll be seen as weak or lacking faith. We secretly believe we should be "over it by now," whatever our "it" might be. But recognizing our wounds takes tremendous courage and is the first step toward genuine healing.

Jesus didn't come just to save our souls for eternity; He came to make us whole right now. And none of this wholeness has anything to do with how good we are able to live a polished life.

In John 10:10, He tells us, "I have come that they may have life, and have it to the full" (NIV). That full life isn't one carefully edited to remove all signs of struggle—it's flourishing in freedom and wholeness.

*When shame tries to keep us silent, we need
to ask ourselves: "Whose voice is really speaking here?"*

Even though God has forgiven us, the accuser—the enemy of our soul—tries to exhaust us with the weight of shame. He doesn't want us to walk in authentic freedom because freed people free people.

When I finally had the courage to share openly about my mental health journey, something unexpected happened. People didn't pull away—they leaned in. They started whispering their own struggles, relieved to know they weren't alone.

My wounded places became gardens where God's healing could reach others who were still sitting in darkness.

So, I challenge you today: Stop plucking away at your imperfections. Stop hiding what hurts. Bring your wounds into God's light where healing can begin.

*Yes, it might feel terrifying at first, but
that temporary discomfort leads to lasting freedom.*

Your transparency isn't just for you—it's for every person who will come after you, walking the same difficult path, believing the lie that they're the only ones struggling. Your courage to speak truth breaks the chains of isolation for countless others.

Remember, we serve a God who specializes in transforming wounded spirits into beautiful blooms.

*Your healing journey begins with a
single, honest step toward Him.*

And I guarantee God wants to use you to shine His glory brightly through your complete story—wilted petals and all. And girl, prepare to bloom spectacularly!

Prayer: Healer of our souls, thank you for seeing our wounds when we try so hard to hide them. Give us courage to stop pretending we're fine and instead bring our hurt into your light where true healing begins. Transform what's broken in us into something beautiful that brings you glory. Help us remember that our most painful experiences can become the source of our most powerful ministry. In Jesus's name, Amen.

growing forward

Tending the Soil
What soul wounds have you been "plucking away" or hiding from others because you think you should be "over them by now"?

Think about the mangled bouquet metaphor. What parts of your story have you been throwing away because you believe they negate all the beauty in your life?

Where has shame kept you silent about your story, and how might God want to use your wounded places to help others who are still sitting in darkness?

Sowing the Seed
Take a moment to identify one area where you've been hiding your pain. Write down a small but brave step toward authentic healing

Rooting in Truth
He heals the brokenhearted and binds up their wounds.
— Psalm 147:3 (NIV)

Branching Out
John 10:10, 2 Corinthians 1:3-4, Isaiah 61:1-3

seeds of thought

sometimes
God lets you see
the favor of opportunity
not to take you to
another place in this world
but simply to take you to
a new level of confidence
in your mind
like scattered seeds
finding soft meadows
where rocky ground
yields wild impossibilities
from single specs
of faithful planting
#barefacedjournals

-day eighteen-
from seeds to meadows

**"The kingdom of heaven is like a mustard seed,
which a man took and planted in His field. Though it
is the smallest of all seeds, yet when it grows, it is the
largest of garden plants and becomes a tree, so that
the birds come and perch in its branches."
—Matthew 13:31-32 (NIV)**

Have you ever marveled at how a single dandelion can
transform an entire lawn? One fluffy seed head caught
in the breeze can scatter dozens of seeds that take root,
grow, and then produce their own seed heads—until
before you know it, what was once a single bloom
becomes a meadow of yellow.

"You take the first step, and I'll multiply the work."
This miracle of multiplication was on my mind during
a challenging spring season when I found myself in a
slump. I was closing in on my fiftieth birthday. I had that
nagging feeling that "life is all downhill from here"—
especially physically. I was stuck.

*But God spoke these words to my heart:
"You take the first step, and I'll multiply the work."*

It reminded me of how wildflowers work. They don't
have to cover the entire field at once. They simply have
to drop one seed, which becomes one bloom, which
scatters more seeds—and God's natural design handles
the multiplication.

*Like a wildflower that doesn't just grow endlessly
but also creates seasons of rest and renewal,
I needed both movement and pause.*

When I shared this nudge with my hubby, Philip, we took it literally. We began going to a nearby botanical garden in the early morning (and I'm NOT a willing morning person). At first, it was a challenge to make it a quarter of the way around the pond without pain. But God continued to whisper: "Amber, take one step, and I'll multiply the work."

So, I made it our goal to walk just to the quarter mark around the pond each day, where a park bench offered sweet renewal. A few weeks into our ritual, while resting at our spot, I said, "God, I believe by summer you'll help me reach halfway around this pond." I set my sights on beautiful Adirondack chairs across the pond, nestled beneath shade trees right by the water.

I told Philip, "I know God will take me halfway around this pond." I couldn't get discouraged in my limitations when I trusted the God of multiplication. Just as a single flower doesn't have to exert itself to fill a field—it simply must be faithful to bloom where it's planted—I only needed to be faithful in taking steps.

*God's economy has always operated on the
principle of multiplication. He is also not someone we
just add in our lives and everything comes up roses.*

The principle of the first seed applies to so many areas of our lives. How often do we find ourselves paralyzed by the enormity of what lies ahead? We see the whole meadow that needs covering—the entire pond to walk around, the mountain to climb, the relationship to rebuild—and we're overwhelmed before we begin.

But God doesn't ask us to cover the entire field at once. he simply invites us to plant one seed, to take one step.

Just one faithful movement in the right direction.
And in that step, something miraculous happens:
God meets us there with His multiplying power.

Think about how wildflowers spread across a landscape. They don't strain or strive. They simply scatter seeds and let nature's design—God's design— do the multiplication work. It's the same throughout Scripture. Moses stretched his staff over the water before it parted. The priests stepped into the Jordan before it stopped flowing. The widow poured her last bit of oil. The little boy handed over his loaves and fishes before the multiplication began.

Plant one seed of faith. Take one step.
He will faithfully multiply the work.

Perhaps you're facing something that seems impossible today. A relationship that needs healing. A calling that seems too big. A dream that feels beyond reach. Or maybe, like me, it's something as simple as a walk that your body rebels against.

Whatever it is, God isn't asking you to fill the whole field or find strength you don't have. Trust Him with that first step today, and watch as he multiplies not just the outcome, but the very strength you need for the journey. And don't forget to rest in the beautiful places He has prepared along the way.

Sometimes the most important part of multiplication is pausing to witness the miracle unfolding around you. And don't forget to rest in the beautiful places he's prepared along the way. Sometimes the most important part of multiplication is pausing to witness the miracle unfolding around you.

Prayer: Heavenly Father, thank you for the miracle of multiplication. Like the mustard seed that grows into a tree where birds find rest, may the small steps of faith I take today be multiplied by your power. When I feel overwhelmed by what lies ahead, remind me that you don't ask me to cover the entire field at once—just to plant one faithful seed. Help me trust in your timing and design, finding rest in the beautiful places you've prepared along my journey. In Jesus's name, Amen

growing forward

Tending the Soil
What "whole field" are you currently feeling
overwhelmed by in your life? How might God be
inviting you to focus on planting just one seed instead?

Like that walk around the pond, what small step of
faith is God asking you to take right now?

Where have you experienced God's multiplication
principle in your life before? How does this give you
courage now?

Sowing the Seed
Take a moment to identify one seemingly impossible
situation in your life. Write down just one small step
you can take this week—your "mustard seed" of faith.
Ask God to multiply your efforts beyond what you can
imagine.

Rooting in Truth
The kingdom of heaven is like a mustard seed, which
a man took and planted in His field. Though it is the
smallest of all seeds, yet when it grows, it is the largest
of garden plants and becomes a tree, so that the birds
come and perch in its branches. —Matthew 13:31-32
(NIV)

Branching Out
Mark 4:30-32, 1 Corinthians 3:6-7, 2 Corinthians 9:10

seeds of thought

seeds of thought

peace is the assurance
of being held securely
knowing you watch over me
even when the landscape changes
even when the storms come
you bring fresh sprouts
to the meadow
you bring the stillness
to the crystal clear streams
#barefacedjournals

-day nineteen-
tending to the pasture

**"The Lord is my shepherd; I shall not want. He
makes me lie down in green pastures. He leads me
beside still waters. He restores my soul."
— Psalm 23:1-3 (ESV)**

In the open pasture, nothing is beyond the shepherd's
care. He doesn't just watch over the sheep—he tends to
the entire landscape that sustains them. The shepherd
knows which hills offer the best protection from winds,
which valleys hold the sweetest water, which fields
produce the most nourishing grass. Even the bugs have
their place in this delicate ecosystem—some pollinating
wildflowers, others aerating the soil, all part of the
intricate balance.

David understood this intimate relationship when
he wrote, "The Lord is MY shepherd." Not simply
someone who keeps me from wandering off, but the
one who tends to the entire landscape of my life—
ensuring that what I need for nourishment, protection,
and rest is provided in just the right measure.

I find such comfort in this image, especially during
seasons when my mind feels scattered and my heart
unsettled.

*The Shepherd isn't just concerned with
my spiritual journey—He cares about the entire
ecosystem of my existence: my mind, my emotions,
my relationships, my physical well-being.*

Nothing is too small for His attention.

The Shepherd tends to both the sheep and the landscape they inhabit with perfect knowledge and care.

One of the most fascinating aspects of shepherding comes from the verse "You anoint my head with oil."

Shepherds would literally pour oil on their sheep's heads to prevent flies from laying eggs in their ears and nasal passages.

Without this protection, the resulting larvae would cause such intense irritation that sheep would sometimes beat their heads against rocks trying to stop the torment even to the point of their own demise.

The shepherd doesn't eliminate all insects from the pasture—an impossible task that would disrupt the ecosystem's balance. Instead, he applies oil precisely where needed, creating a protective barrier against specific threats while allowing beneficial insects to continue their important work in the landscape.

What a powerful picture of how God tends to the landscape of our minds! He doesn't remove every difficulty—anxiety, sadness, and stress are natural parts of the human experience, just as insects are natural parts of a pasture. But He does provide protective "oil" for specific threats that could cause lasting damage if left unaddressed.

I've come to see my mental health journey through this lens. The same Shepherd who leads me beside still waters also provides the oil that protects my mind from harm.

Sometimes that oil comes through therapy or medication. Sometimes it's found in community, boundaries, or rest. Whatever form it takes, it's part of how He tends to the entire landscape of my being.

I used to think taking medication for mental health meant I lacked faith. But I've come to recognize that the Shepherd uses many tools to tend His pasture—rain and sunshine, staff and rod, still waters and protective oil. Each serves its purpose in the landscape He's carefully cultivating.

When I feel overwhelmed, when anxiety buzzes around me like those bothersome flies, I remember that the Shepherd knows every inch of the landscape of my life.

He sees the hidden springs beneath dry ground. He knows where new growth waits to emerge. He understands which challenges help me grow stronger and which threats need His protective intervention.

That medication bottle on your nightstand? It might be part of how the Shepherd tends to the landscape of your mind. That therapy appointment? Perhaps it's the still waters where healing begins.

That boundary you're learning to set? It could be the Shepherd's rod, keeping predators from destroying what He's cultivating.

In the pasture of God's care, nothing is overlooked. The sheep receive individual attention while the landscape itself is nurtured—creating an environment where both the flock, the wildflowers, and yes, even the bugs fulfill their greater purpose in the larger picture of His design.

Prayer: Tender Shepherd, thank You for tending to the entire landscape of my life with such detailed care. You know what I need before I can even ask. When harmful thoughts buzz around me, anoint me with Your protective oil. When my spirit thirsts, lead me to still waters. Help me trust that Your care extends to every aspect of who I am—from the broad pastures to the smallest wildflower, from the refreshing streams to even the bugs that serve their purpose in Your design. In Jesus's name, Amen.

growing forward

Tending the Soil
What areas in the landscape of your life need the Shepherd's particular attention right now?

How have you seen God tend to your mental and emotional landscape in the past?

What challenges in your current landscape might actually be serving a purpose in your growth?

Sowing the Seed
Think of your life as a pasture under the Shepherd's care. Identify three specific areas: one place that needs still waters, one that needs protective oil, and one that needs green pastures. Write down one practical step to receive the Shepherd's landscape-tending care in each area this week.

Rooting in Truth
"The Lord is my shepherd; I shall not want. He makes me lie down in green pastures. He leads me beside still waters. He restores my soul." —Psalm 23:1-3 (ESV)

Branching Out
John 10:11-14, Philippians 4:6-7, Isaiah 26:3

seeds of thought

seeds of thought

seeds take flight
on invisible currents
white wisps
breaking free
from their moorings
unapologtic in their
take to the wind
or where they end up
to root anew in
the solid of foundations
the beauties in prairies
the yellows of glory
to proudly gaze up
#barefacedjournals

-day twenty-
floating on the breeze

**"Each of you should use whatever gift you have
received to serve others, as faithful stewards of
God's grace in its various forms."
—1 Peter 4:10 (NIV)**

I never expected to find ministry in 260 pounds of
fur, drool, and boundless enthusiasm. Yet Stuart and
Stanley, my family's Great Pyrenees duo, have become
living lessons in how beauty scatters in the most
unexpected ways.

With windows down and spring air flowing, we drive
through town as their pristine white fur creates our own
version of dandelion season—countless tiny messengers
of joy carried on the breeze.

We take them on walks through the local botanical
garden. Their fluffy white fur catches the morning
breeze, flying with the breeze to find their place among
the pristine botanicals at the park. We find it the next
day floating in the lake, caught between the leaves of
shade plants, even decorating the formal beds. The
gardeners probably didn't plan for "Pyrenees accents"
in their landscape design, but I like to think it adds a
certain whimsical charm.

*Because of these guys, I've learned that sometimes the
most powerful ministry doesn't come with a pulpit or a
platform. Sometimes it comes with white floating fluff.*

I've learned that ministry isn't about creating perfect

conditions. It's about blooming exactly where you're planted—even if it's in a minivan with dog hair everywhere.

No matter how many holes they dig, how many socks they drag across the yard, how much fur decorates my coffee, I can't help but laugh.

> These giant floof-balls are living proof that ministry doesn't require a perfectly delivered sermon—it just requires presence.

My favorite part? Watching stressed-out faces transform when we pull up. Young, old—doesn't matter. Something about these ridiculous, slobbery creatures breaks through not only the concrete of my daily frustration, but many others they come in contact with. They're like unexpected wildflowers spreading unexpected joy just by being seen.

We've taken them to my husband's workplace during the holiday rush—a living, breathing stress-reduction system. All because sometimes ministry looks like a hug. Sometimes it comes with fur and drool. Sometimes it looks like nothing you'd expect.

My mother understood this. She was the "Reverend of Clean Laundry," transforming her senior living community with something as simple as perfectly folded towels. Her gift wasn't grand. It was faithful. It was love in motion.

> What seemingly small gift are you hiding from the world? What seeds of fluff are you keeping tucked away, thinking they're not impressive enough to share?

What seemingly mundane thing are you holding back? The ability to bake a pie? To change a tire? To write a poem? To simply show up? God doesn't measure ministry by its impressiveness. He measures it by its heart.

First Peter reminds us that our gifts come in VARIOUS FORMS. There's no prerequisite. No credential required. Just a willingness to let what you love become a conduit for God's goodness.

His love + your gifts = His glory shining through.

These persistent blooms of joy—whether they're dogs, or pies, or perfectly folded laundry—they're how God's light breaks through. Not always dramatically. Sometimes just by showing up, fur and all.

The world doesn't need more perfect people.
It needs more people willing to scatter joy
in whatever messy, beautiful way they can.

It's time to take your place. Not as someone with a perfect plan, but as someone willing to bloom where you're planted. To let your unique gifts and blessings scatter like seeds, never knowing exactly where they might take root.

Prayer: Father, forgive me for holding back the gifts you've given me. Help me see the ministry in my everyday moments. Give me courage to bloom exactly where I am, to spread joy in ways only I can. Remind me that your love works through the most unexpected carriers—even fluffy, slobbery ones. In Jesus's name, Amen.

growing forward

Tending the Soil

1. What seemingly ordinary gift, talent, or passion do you have that brings others joy?

2. What's one small way you could use that gift this week as a "ministry of presence"?

3. What fears or insecurities have kept you from sharing your unique gifts with others?

Sowing the Seed

Think of someone whose simple, everyday actions have brought joy to your life. Write them a note of appreciation this week, letting them know how their "ordinary ministry" has impacted you.

Rooting in Truth

"Each of you should use whatever gift you have received to serve others, as faithful stewards of God's grace in its various forms." 1 Peter 4:10 (NIV)

Branching Out

Romans 12:6-8, Matthew 5:14-16, Ephesians 2:10

seeds of thought

i have yet to see
the darkness dictate
a seed's ability
to find its way up
#barefacedjournals

-day twenty-one-
surviving alaska winter

In my distress I prayed to the LORD,
and the LORD answered me and set me free.
—Psalm 118:5 (NLT)

I've always been fascinated by those Alaskan winters—
you know, the ones where the sun barely shows its
face for months at a time? In Barrow, one of Alaska's
northernmost cities, the sun actually sets in mid-
November and doesn't rise again until mid-January.
That's complete darkness for two whole months. Can
you imagine living in that kind of persistent night? It
sounds like the perfect metaphor for those seasons of
our lives when hope feels distant and God seems silent.

But here's the thing that blows my mind:
plants still grow there. In Alaska. In the dark.

As the days shorten and cold sets in, these incredible
plants begin to "harden" themselves. They pump water
out of their cells into their roots, and the remaining
sugary sap acts like an antifreeze. What's even more
remarkable is that for many plants, snow actually
provides insulation—creating pockets of air that protect
against harsh winds and freezing temperatures, like a
natural igloo.

When Philip and I were walking through our own
Alaskan winter of grief—losing his dad and then his
brother just a month later, all while the pandemic

was unfolding—I remember lying in bed one night, surrounded by shadows both in our room and in our hearts. The weight of loss felt suffocating, like we were buried under feet of snow with no sunlight in sight.

That's when I whispered to him, "This feels like the end of the world. It's hard to imagine that anything will ever be OK again. But do you know what the best thing about bleak times?"

His response came softly through the darkness: "Jesus...because I don't know how we could deal with all this without Him."

There it was—our sunlight in the bleak of winter, a bloom pushing through the overwhelming feelings of hopelessness. Not a dismissal of our pain, but the recognition that even in the darkest places, life and light can break through.

When plants in Alaska face temperatures 24 degrees below zero, they don't just give up and die. They adapt. They transform. They create systems to prevent ice crystals from forming and damaging their cells. I think we humans could learn something profound from their quiet resilience.

You know, being set free by God doesn't mean our situations change instantly. It means we are freed from being defined by our situations. Like those Alaskan plants, we can develop our own spiritual antifreeze—prayer, community, worship, Scripture, simply learning to be still in His presence—that keeps us alive during the bleakest of seasons.

Plants modify their life cycles and growth rates to deal with changing seasons and lack of moisture. In our darkest times, we might need to do the same—slowing down, conserving emotional energy, drawing from the nutrients we stored during brighter seasons.

And here's the miracle: when Alaskan plants finally feel that spring sunlight again after months of darkness, they don't just survive—they thrive. People in Alaska report experiencing what locals call "spring mania" when the sunlight finally returns—unusual happiness and renewed energy after the long dark.

There's wisdom in winter. There's purpose in the dark. There's growth happening underground that we can't see.

So if you're in an Alaskan season right now, remember this: just because you can't see the sun doesn't mean it's gone forever. Just because you feel buried doesn't mean you've been abandoned. Father knows exactly what you need to grow through this season.

And trust me on this: when you reach for His light even in the darkest place, you'll feel a peace that's downright unreasonable, a love so overwhelming it seems to crush all the darkness in its embrace.

Jesus is here, right here, in the thick of it all with us. Not erasing our problems but empowering us to face them with a strength that isn't our own, helping us grow and reach for the light in ways we never thought possible.

Like those resilient Alaskan plants, you already have everything you need in Him to survive this winter. And when spring comes—and it will come—you'll bloom in ways you never imagined possible.

Prayer: Father, in these seasons when the light seems so far away, remind me that You're still at work. Like those plants that grow in the Alaskan darkness, help me to develop spiritual resilience that can withstand the harshest conditions. Thank You that my identity isn't determined by the darkness around me but by Your light within me. In Jesus's name, Amen.

growing forward

Tending the Soil
1. What "dark season" are you experiencing right now, and how has it affected your spiritual life?

2. What spiritual "antifreeze" has God provided to help you survive difficult seasons?

3. What unexpected growth might be happening in your life right now, even though you can't see it yet?

Sowing the Seed
Take a moment to write down three things you're grateful for even in this dark season. Choose one of these to focus on each day this week as a reminder of God's presence.

Rooting in Truth
"In my distress I prayed to the LORD, and the LORD answered me and set me free." — Psalm 118:5 (NLT)

Branching Out
Isaiah 43:2, Romans 5:3-5, James 1:2-4

seeds of thought

fragrant hope holds the space
where grace drips like nectar
and love blooms unexpected
in the spaces between
what we can and cannot see
just waiting for me
to open my hands
and freely receive it
#barefacedjournals

-day twenty-two-
the aroma of attraction

But thanks be to God, who always leads us in triumphal procession in Christ and through us spreads everywhere the fragrance of the knowledge of Him. — 2 Corinthians 2:14 (NIV)

I've always been a sucker for the smell of fresh oranges. That burst of citrusy brightness that hits you the moment you peel back the skin—it's an instant mood lifter.

Growing up, the holiday season held a special memory of orange-smelling goodness for me. My Uncle Ron would send us a box of oranges from Florida almost every December, and I swear those fruits were magic.

One slice, and the entire kitchen would transform into this vibrant, sun-filled sanctuary of pure joy.

But that's the thing I love most about citrus: its power isn't just in looking pretty. It's in its ability to fill an entire space with its presence.

Just like that one orange can make a whole room smell uplifting, as Christ-followers we're called to be those unexpected bursts of hope that change the atmosphere wherever we go—drawing people in to its source.

I'm gonna be honest—sometimes I've worried about "doing ministry right." I've stressed about the perfect words, worried if I didn't have a Bible verse memorized for every occasion—like I was a contestant on "Jeopardy: Bible Edition." I've felt less-than if people knew I didn't spend hours praying and having devotions, as if I somehow lacked in my spiritual walk.

But what if attraction to Christ is less about performing and more about simply being—like an orange tree that can't help but release its fragrance?

Jesus didn't hand out instruction manuals. He just lived. And people were drawn to Him not because He was perfect, but because He was authentically present.

The crazy part? We're not supposed to manufacture this attraction. We're just supposed to be fully ourselves, fully saturated in God's love. Like that orange tree that doesn't try to smell good—it just does, because that's its nature.

Sometimes we get so worried about not "spoiling the fruit" that we forget the whole point of fruit is to be consumed, to nourish, to give life.

The fruits of the Spirit aren't about looking pristine on a shelf. They're about being bruised, broken open, and releasing something life-giving.

I've watched oranges sit on my kitchen table and completely lose their taste, or worse yet, grow mushy and moldy. It happens so easily in my house—someone buys them with the best intentions, but then everyone's rushing through their 30-minute lunch breaks, and nobody wants to take the time to peel one.

I wonder if that happens to us too, when we hold back our gifts, when we refuse to be broken open and used.

We were never meant to sit pristine and protected on display. We were meant to be shared, to be poured out. To be His diffuser of love, grace, and forgiveness.

In fact, something even more amazing happens to oranges that are pressed and diffused— they become even more potent. Did you know that the oil from orange peels contains something called d-limonene—a compound that can boost your immune system, reduce inflammation, and even lift your mood?

What's amazing is that this healing property only gets released when the orange is broken open, when pressure is applied to the rind. The very thing that protects the fruit becomes its most powerful gift when it's surrendered.

Orange essential oil is incredibly concentrated—just a few drops can change an entire room. It has the power to cut through grime and dissolve what's stuck. It can clear away residue that nothing else seems to touch.

In the same way, when we allow ourselves to be vessels of God's presence, we become carriers of something that can dissolve shame, cut through despair, and clear away the residue of hopelessness in the lives around us.

Just as an orange carries immunity-boosting properties hidden in its skin, you carry healing properties too— kindness that strengthens others' emotional immune systems, truth that fights against deception, love that overcomes division. But these properties only get released when you're willing to be pressed, to be broken open, to let what's inside you flow outward to those who need it most.

I think that's what Paul meant when he talked about being the fragrance of Christ. It's not about performing religious duties or checking spiritual boxes. It's about allowing the authentic essence of who we are—who He's made us to be—to permeate every space we enter. It's about carrying healing properties that others can benefit from, simply by being near us.

*You don't need to be everywhere or help everyone.
You just need to be fully present where you are,
allowing your God-given essence to diffuse
His love naturally to those around you.*

And sometimes the aroma of the smallest gestures
of fruitfulness— love, joy, peace, patience, kindness,
goodness, faithfulness, gentleness and self-control—
create the most lasting impact.

*Prayer: Father, help me be a fragrant offering. Not
perfect, but present. Not performing, but simply being
saturated in Your love. Like the essential oil of an orange
that carries healing properties, let my life carry Your
presence in ways that bring health and hope to others.
Let my life be like a burst of unexpected citrus—bringing
joy, healing, and a hint of Your incredible grace wherever
I go. In Jesus's name, Amen.*

growing forward

Tending the Soil
1. Where have you been trying to manufacture spiritual attraction instead of simply being?

2. What has God been cultivating in your life right now that can draw people to you—hospitality, compassion, a joyful spirit?

3. How can you be more authentically focused on your power to transform the atmosphere as you carry the fragrance of Christ everywhere you go?

Sowing the Seed
Find something fragrant today—an orange, a candle, a flower. As you enjoy its scent, ask God to make your life similarly attractive to others, not through performance, but through genuine love. If possible, use a drop of orange essential oil on your wrists as a reminder throughout the day of the impact your life can make.

Rooting in Truth
But thanks be to God, who always leads us in triumphal procession in Christ and through us spreads everywhere the fragrance of the knowledge of Him.
— 2 Corinthians 2:14 (NIV)

Branching Out
Galatians 5:22-23, John 15:4-5, Philippians 4:18

seeds of thought

seeds of thought

let the breeze take its toll
pushing the branch's bend
let me find the sway of the dance
and delight in the slap of the rain
the roll off my hard skins
let the refresh soak me to the core
find the grounding for deep roots
let me stand tall
a steady platform for the birds
as they push their babies
to find first flight
let me be the safety
to keep the predators at bay
and the dependable shade
#barefacedjournals

-day twenty-three-
scattered seed in shifting soil

"We have this hope as an anchor for the soul, firm and secure." — Hebrews 6:19 (NIV)

Botanists have a term for plants that thrive in challenging environments: extremophiles. They're the living miracles that find a way to grow where nothing should survive—clinging to mountain cliffs, nestled in arctic tundra, emerging from volcanic landscapes. My spiritual journey has felt exactly like that—a persistent attempt to find growth in seemingly impossible terrain.

I've learned that hope isn't about perfect conditions. It's about radical adaptation.

There's a tiny flower called the snow gentian that blooms in the harshest alpine environments. When most plants would surrender, it unfurls delicate petals against winds that could easily crush it.

Its root system is a marvel of engineering—shallow, yet incredibly intricate, spreading out just beneath the surface to capture every possible nutrient, every hint of moisture.

My most challenging seasons have looked remarkably similar. Mental health struggles that felt like continuous winter. Ministry disappointments that threatened to uproot everything I believed. Moments when hope seemed as fragile as those alpine blooms, yet somehow persisted.

I've watched these extremophile plants
through documentaries and drives through the desert.
They don't just survive—they reveal something
profound about resilience.

They don't ask permission. They don't wait for their circumstances to be better. They simply grow.

The biblical heroes understood this long before modern botany. Abraham traveling to an unknown land. Moses leading a nation through a desert. Mary accepting a calling that would change everything. They weren't guaranteed success. They were guaranteed something far more important: God's persistent presence.

Christ's promise isn't about removing obstacles. It's about providing sustenance in the midst of them. "Do not let your hearts be troubled" —He even says these words twice. (See John 14:1, John 14:27.) It's an invitation to develop a root system deeper than our current circumstances.

In my own life, hope has worked like those
alpine plants. Not a loud, triumphant declaration.
But a quiet, persistent reaching.

Sometimes just millimeters of growth. Sometimes just maintaining connection when everything else suggests giving up.

I think about the mycorrhizal networks underground— those incredible fungal connections that help trees communicate and support each other. Even when a single tree seems isolated, an entire hidden network is providing nutrients, warning of dangers, sharing resources.

Our hope works similarly. We're never truly alone,
even when we feel most disconnected.

Some of God's most significant work happens in the seasons we can't see. Where roots are developing. Where unseen support systems are establishing themselves. Where hope is less about what we can observe and more about what we choose to believe. We aren't just hoping for ourselves. We become living testimonies. Those unexpected blooms revealing that something miraculous is always possible, even when the ground feels unstable.

Prayer: Father, when my hope feels fragile, remind me that You are the master gardener. Help me trust the seed You've planted, even when the soil shifts beneath me. Teach me to keep reaching, to keep growing, to keep believing—not in my own strength, but in your persistent love. Anchor me in your promises when everything else feels uncertain. Show me the hidden networks of grace supporting me, even when I cannot see them. In Jesus's name, Amen.

growing forward

Tending the Soil
When have you had to adapt to "shifting soil" in your spiritual journey?

What "extremophile" qualities has God developed in you through difficult seasons?

How might your current challenges be developing a deeper root system in your life?

Sowing the Seed
Take time this week to journal about a specific challenge you're facing. Instead of focusing on when it will end, ask: "What adaptation might God be developing in me through this season?" Consider how this difficulty might actually be strengthening your spiritual root system.

Rooting in Truth
"We have this hope as an anchor for the soul, firm and secure." — Hebrews 6:19 (NIV)

Branching Out
Romans 5:3-5, James 1:2-4, 2 Corinthians 4:16-18

seeds of thought

section four

EMBRACING
NEW LANDSCAPES

wildflowers need
to wander

***Embracing fresh callings, unexpected joy, and the
beautiful ways God transforms our journey beyond
what we could ever imagine.***

learn to appreciate the life
right in front of your face
in every inch of quiet space
in every giggle
set your mind solid
to circle thankful
for what you have
and your have nots
for lack is blind to itself
until it is measured by
greener fields and
greater expectations
in a day's ripe harvest
every goodness is on the table
if we'd only open our eyes
on each new sunrise to pay
love forward and
feast on the riches
#barefacedjournals

-day twenty-four-
the canopy of contentment

"I have learned in whatever situation I am to be content. I know how to be brought low, and I know how to abound. In any and every circumstance, I have learned the secret of facing plenty and hunger, abundance and need." —Philippians 4:11-12 (ESV)

I love sitting out in my backyard around my firepit staring up at the trees above it, and my family knows why I cherish this simple luxury. Every night I have the opportunity, I just sit beside the flames, surrounded by trees, toasting a big fat campfire marshmallow in my little nook in the backyard that I overlooked for many years.

It's amazing the way contentment transforms ordinary moments into extraordinary experiences—creating abundance where others might just see the everyday.

And I do what I always do—sit quietly in gratitude, recognizing that the richest treasures aren't waiting in some distant place but right here in front of me.

Those bends of flickering light consistently remind me that no matter what is happening outside my nook, I can release the strife of a hectic day in this God-given space where peace and contentment is surrounding me.

That's how contentment works—not denying the existence of greater things, but fully experiencing the beauty of what's already yours.

But there's a phenomenon that has seeped into our "Amazon" fixated society. Did you know there's fascinating research about this? Studies show that most of us get more excited about waiting for online purchases than in-store ones. Scientists discovered that dopamine—that feel-good chemical in our brains—doesn't surge when we get the reward. Instead, dopamine causes you to want, desire, seek out, and search. The real pleasure is in the anticipation, the journey toward what we desire.

But here's what struck me—we've been treating contentment all wrong. We think it's about having everything we want right now. But real contentment is about learning to enjoy the waiting itself, finding joy in the journey rather than constantly rushing to the next destination.

Sometimes I've gotten caught in that temptation too—especially when focused on the next new thing I want to acquire.

> *Ambition is a crazy thing, right? It whispers that satisfaction is always on the other side of the next achievement.*

I've felt that pull toward "if only"—believing that fulfillment required different circumstances for more impressive surroundings than my "west side of the city zipcode" For years I had cataloged all the ways I didn't measure up to others' standards. When I finally had my breakthrough moment sitting beneath those trees with flames flickering, everything shifted—not my address, but my perspective. .

> *The world teaches us to seek the impressive, aspire to better neighborhoods and never settle. After all, shouldn't our surroundings reflect our worth?*

What I've come to realize is that contentment isn't about settling for less – it's about recognizing the extraordinary value in what we already have.

It's about training our eyes to see beauty where others might only see limitations. It's transforming our perspective about what makes our current situation valuable, rather than constantly looking elsewhere for fulfillment.

Jesus didn't promise that happiness comes from acquisition or achievement; He consistently reminded us to find peace in recognizing what's already been provided. "Do not store up for yourselves treasures on earth, where moths and vermin destroy, and where thieves break in and steal. But store up for yourselves treasures in heaven," He tells us in Matthew 6:19-20.

That abundant life isn't dependent on having more or better—it's flourishing through recognizing the eternal value of the gifts we've already been given right where we are.

When I embraced the joy of my backyard firepit, something unexpected happened. People weren't drawn to impressive surroundings—they were drawn to the authentic contentment they found there. They started sharing their own exhaustion from constantly chasing "more" and "better," relieved to discover that meaningful joy doesn't require attaining the next thing on their wish list.

So, I challenge you today: Stop believing the lie that contentment requires that next promotion, or a better car, or that recognition you've deserved for many years.

I promise God wants to use you to display his transforming perspective magnificently through your story—backyard firepit and all. And girl, prepare to shine like diamonds while others are still exhausting themselves chasing after illusions of wealth.

The canopy of trees above my firepit isn't impressive by Instagram standards. But it's MY canopy, where God meets me—and under His covering, I've found the kind of contentment that Amazon will never have the capacity to deliver.

Prayer: Source of living water, thank you for offering nourishment when we feel depleted. Give us wisdom to plant our roots by your streams instead of trying to survive on our own strength. Transform our weary souls into sheltering canopies that reflect your unfailing care. Help us remember that our most challenging seasons can become the source of our most meaningful ministry to others. In Jesus's name, Amen.

growing forward

Tending the Soil
Where in your life are you constantly looking for "the next thing" instead of appreciating what you have?

What ordinary blessing in your life might become extraordinary if you viewed it through the lens of contentment?

How has your pursuit of "more" or "better" affected your ability to enjoy the present?

Sowing the Seed
This week, create a "contentment practice": Each day, sit for 5 minutes in a place you normally overlook (like a backyard, a corner of your home, or even your car), and write down three specific things about this ordinary space that bring you joy. Notice how this practice shifts your perspective over time.

Rooting in Truth
"I have learned in whatever situation I am to be content. I know how to be brought low, and I know how to abound." —Philippians 4:11-12 (ESV)

Branching Out
Matthew 6:19-21, 1 Timothy 6:6-8, Hebrews 13:5

seeds of thought

seeds of thought

silent softness
i am in need of you
a cove of quiet plush
where i come back to my senses
push a cool glass to my brow
help me escape
the heat pressing my back
and the noise of loud minds
give me the shade of tall trees
in the sink of a hammock's resting
to rock away
a day's worry
wisping cloudy pictures
in the sky
#barefacedjournals

-day twenty-five-
lessons from the lily pad

"Come to me, all you who are weary and burdened, and I will give you rest." —Matthew 11:28 (NIV)

Have you ever watched a water lily? I mean really watched one—not just glanced at it in passing, but sat and observed how it exists in its environment? Water lilies understand something about rest that I'm still learning. Anchored deep beneath the surface, they float effortlessly—unbothered by the water's turbulence, their broad leaves spread wide, absorbing sunlight without straining.

I've spent most of my life doing the opposite. Thrashing. Struggling. Believing rest was something to be earned rather than received. Each task another weight pulling me under, another reason why I couldn't possibly stop and breathe.

The lily pad doesn't fight the water. It doesn't try to swim against the current or prove its worth by constant motion. It simply exists. Rooted. Supported. Peaceful.

How often do we feel like we need to be in constant motion? Our culture celebrates the "hustle" and glorifies exhaustion as if it were a badge of honor. "I'm so busy" has become our default response when someone asks how we're doing.

We've convinced ourselves that our value is tied to our productivity—that if we're not constantly producing, achieving, or creating, we're somehow falling behind.

When Jesus encountered the man by the healing pool at Bethesda, He saw through years of exhausted striving. "Do you want to get well?" He asked. Not, "How hard have you tried?" Not, "What elaborate plan have you developed?" Simply, "Do you want healing?"

The man had been stuck for thirty-eight years. Thirty-eight years of making excuses. Thirty-eight years of believing his healing depended on his own effort.

Sound familiar?

I wonder how many of us have been lying by our own poolsides, watching others receive their healing while we clutch our excuses close to our chests. "I don't have anyone to help me." "Someone always gets there first." "I've tried everything." We've become so accustomed to our limitations that we've built our identities around them.

Those lily pads teach me something profound about spiritual rest. They're deeply rooted, yet they float. They're anchored, yet flexible. They absorb light without fighting for it. They rest without guilt.

Our productivity-driven world screams that rest is laziness. That constant motion equals worth.

But God places more value on our reliance on Him than on our résumés. He invites us to float—to be supported, to be held, to be at peace. Jesus didn't say, "Come to me when you've finished your to-do list" or "Come to me once you've proven your worth." He simply said, "Come."

The more things we accumulate—possessions, achievements, obligations—the more weights we're attaching to our souls. They're just concrete blocks keeping us from floating, anchoring us to the bottom of the pool instead of allowing us to rise to the surface where we can breathe.

> *Your breakthrough might look like surrender.*
> *Like choosing presence over productivity. Like allowing*
> *yourself to be carried instead of constantly swimming.*

I'm learning to be more like the lily pad. To stop fighting the current. To trust that I'm held by something deeper than my own efforts. To believe that my value isn't determined by my output but by the One who created me.

> *No one can float for you. No one can bring the healing*
> *waters to you. But they're there. Waiting. Inviting.*

Will you join me at the lily pad today?

Prayer: Father, I'm tired of fighting the current. Tired of proving my worth through constant motion. Today, I choose to float in your grace. Root me deeply in your love, so I can rest lightly on the surface of your peace. Help me release the weights of my own expectations and the pressure to constantly produce. Teach me the wisdom of the lily pad—to be both anchored and free. In Jesus's name, Amen.

growing forward

Tending the Soil
What areas of your life do you feel the most pressure to constantly "do" rather than simply "be"?

What excuses have you been making that prevent you from accepting God's invitation to rest?

How might your relationships, work, or spiritual life change if you learned to "float" more and "swim" less?

Sowing the Seed
Make a list of three "weights" you're carrying that prevent you from experiencing true rest. Next to each one, write a simple action you can take this week to begin releasing that weight. Consider sharing this list with a trusted friend who can hold you accountable.

Rooting in Truth
"Come to me, all you who are weary and burdened, and I will give you rest." —Matthew 11:28 (NIV)

Branching Out
Psalm 46:10, Isaiah 30:15, Hebrews 4:9-11

seeds of thought

tender stems
find daylight
against all expectation
a reminder that beneath
the hardest surfaces
life waits patiently
for its moment
to declare hope
in visible form
each sprig emerges
a testament to unseen work
and certain promise
that what God begins
he surely completes
#barefacedjournals

-day twenty-six-
sprouts of promise

"And we know that in all things God works for the good of those who love Him, who have been called according to his purpose." — Romans 8:28 (NIV)

We live in an old 1950s ranch house—just 1,200 square feet—that we've called home for over 25 years. We bought our 3-bedroom house in 1999 then as life unfolded, as kids happened, we only tended to the emergency house fixes.

You know how it goes—the roof leaks, the furnace quits, the water heater gives out. Those take priority, and the "nice-to-have" updates get pushed to someday.

For all those years, our home hadn't seen any exterior updates, and I've been genuinely content with the goodness I've been given. Yet there were moments recently when I thought, "This will not happen." Each time, my doubt was overturned by my step to just believe God has a complete refreshment for overlooked and undervalued spaces in my life.

I'm definitely not someone who believes that simply declaring I want something means God will automatically give me things.

I never want to treat Him like a supernatural vending machine—He's so much more than just a giver of good things

But I've prayed about these spaces, knowing that

someday... maybe... I'd see the bigger picture unfold into something more abundant than I thought possible because I know he has the provision already set up for to do what only he can do as we put our trust in Him.

> I don't know about you, but there's no way
> I can carry the weight of day-to-day needs—
> especially those that pop up unexpectedly. So,
> I've started reprogramming my mind to say
> "within your means, Father." I know you'll show up to
> complete the work that's been started.

Let me share a miracle that happened recently. City utilities came to move our street gas lines down to lay new water line. I joked—"You can remove the old driveway that used to be in front of our old attached garage—and you can remove the cracked path in front of my old flower bed too."

To my surprise, they said, "Sure we'll do that—and we are going to come back and put grass seed down."

Even when they laid the seed down, I didn't expect much. The ground was packed hard from years of gravel and vehicle and foot traffic. The weather forecast showed days of tornadic wind coming—not ideal conditions for new grass seed. But God had other plans.

> Today I'm seeing a lawn that was decimated
> find sprouts despite many days of
> flooding rain and tornadic wind.

I was so amazed by this little sprigs of green, I had to take a picture and share it on social media. I am convinced, this is what God is rolling out on a larger scale in the lives of his children.

This is what YOU need to believe for your life today. If you've been waiting for movement—if you've been staring at hard-packed soil wondering if anything could ever grow there—find and take a picture of some sprouting foliage for your mind to frame because what He is doing for me He is doing for YOU!

> *Take time to look closer at the ground today, and notice the sprouts of His good promises rising to the surface.*

It's just the beginning. I'm believing He will finish the work, just because I will never forget where it started, moreover Who started it.

We often want the full bloom, the complete transformation, but God wants us to celebrate each stage of growth. Each little sprout is evidence of His faithfulness.

Prayer: Father, help me to see the tiny sprouts of your promises in my life. Renew my faith when I'm tempted to doubt, and give me patience as I wait for your complete provision. Thank you for working within your means, not mine. Help me to trust your timing and celebrate each small sign of growth along the way. Amen.

growing forward

Tending the Soil
Where are the overlooked and undervalued spaces in
your life that God might be wanting to refresh?

How can you step into belief rather than doubt
regarding His provision?

What unexpected provisions from God have you
experienced recently that you might have overlooked?

Sowing the Seed
Take a moment to identify one "sprouting promise" in
your life—something small that God is growing. Write
it down and thank Him specifically for this sign of His
faithfulness. Then share this sprouting promise with
someone else who might need encouragement today.

Rooting in Truth
"And we know that in all things God works for the good
of those who love Him, who have been called according
to his purpose." —Romans 8:28 (NIV)

Branching Out
Isaiah 43:19, Matthew 13:31-32, Zechariah 4:10

seeds of thought

my soul blooms in
the light of you
and my song
is your heartbeat
#barefacedjournals

-day twenty-seven-
survivor: twig in my yard edition

"Being confident of this, that he who began a good work in you will carry it on to completion until the day of Christ Jesus." — Philippians 1:6 NIV

I'm not trying to have the perfect lawn. I just don't want it to look like an abandoned house is lurking behind those random sticks sprouting everywhere.

Most of those sticks from the front yard? Gone. Cut down. Cleared out. I'm not about that overgrown, forgotten yard life. But one stick—just one—survived my landscaping purge. Philip saw something in that single twig that I completely missed.

"Leave it," he'd say. And somehow, against all my yard maintenance plans, that one stick remained.

Now it stands a towering tree, bursting with blossoms every spring—a living, breathing testament to the fact that God is always doing something, even when we can't see it. While all the other sticks met their end, this one became something extraordinary.

I've learned that life is rarely about keeping everything neat. It's about recognizing potential in the most unexpected places. That stick that looked like nothing? It was the beginning of something beautiful.

My life has been full of moments that looked like random, unwanted growth. Seasons that felt like interruptions. Experiences I was sure were going nowhere. But somehow, God kept whispering, "Not yet. I'm not finished."

Have you ever stood in the middle of what feels like a complete mess, wondering if anything good could possibly come from it? Maybe it's a career detour that seems to be leading nowhere. Perhaps it's a relationship that's taking an unexpected turn. Or maybe it's just life happening in all its chaotic, unplanned glory when you'd prefer a little more order.

We live in a culture obsessed with overnight success stories. We would all love the "before and after" without all the mess in the middle.

But the truth is, growth rarely follows our preferred timeline. That "stick" in my yard didn't transform overnight. For months—years, actually—it just looked like an eyesore. Just a forgotten twig that someone forgot to remove. Nothing special. Nothing promising. Nothing worth mentioning.

I think about how many times I've been tempted to "clean up" areas of my life that seemed messy or unproductive. How many dreams I've abandoned because they weren't developing fast enough. How many relationships I've nearly walked away from because they weren't immediately perfect. How many times I've told God, "This can't possibly be part of your plan."

Spiritual growth isn't about dramatic transformations. It's about those tiny, almost imperceptible moments of choosing to believe. Choosing to hope. Choosing to take one more breath when everything suggests giving up.

Do you ever wonder how many "sticks" you've cut down in your own life? How many potential blessings you've cleared away because they didn't meet your expectations for how they should look?

I know I've done it. We're so quick to label things
as failures, interruptions, or mistakes when they're
actually just beginnings that don't look like beginnings
yet.

I don't know what looks like a disposable 'stick' in
your life right now. Maybe it's a dream that feels out
of place. Maybe it's a relationship that seems like an
unexpected interruption. Maybe it's your own sense
of purpose, feeling as random and unplanned as that
lone random stick in the landscape in your mind's eye.

But here's what I'm learning: God specializes in
the overlooked. The unexpected. The things we're
absolutely certain don't belong.

Breaking through doesn't always look impressive.
Sometimes it looks like the landscape
that is only suited for an abandoned house.

Sometimes it's just deciding to breathe for one more
day. Sometimes it's reaching for the tiniest sliver of
light when everything else feels dark. Sometimes it's
simply allowing yourself to grow exactly where you've
been planted.

There's a beautiful passage in Zechariah 4:10 that
asks, "Who dares despise the day of small beginnings?"
That question has haunted me.

How many times have I despised—or at least
dismissed—the small beginnings in my own life?

How many times have I failed to see the potential
in what God was doing because it didn't match my
expectations of what growth should look like?

The truth is, God rarely works in the dramatic,
overnight transformations we crave. More often, He
works in the slow, steady process of becoming—in the

almost invisible moments of faithfulness when no one else is watching.

Your timeline won't look like anyone else's. Your growth might be slower. More complicated. Less picture-perfect. But it's no less sacred.

Sometimes the most beautiful transformations happen in the spaces where we're tempted to give up on.

In the moments when we're ready to cut down that "stick" because we can't possibly see how it could ever become anything worthwhile.

One day—and trust me on this—you'll look back and see how something beautiful was forming all along.

You'll realize that what once seemed like yard clutter was actually an invitation to witness something greater—something miraculous.

Because that's who our God is. He's the God who takes the overlooked and makes it extraordinary. The God who sees potential where we see only mess. The God who promises to complete the good work He began in you—even when that work doesn't look anything like what you expected.

Prayer: Father, forgive me for wanting to clear away the "sticks" in my life. Help me trust that You're always working, even when I can't see it. Give me eyes to see potential where I see only mess. Remind me that your most profound work often begins in the spaces I'm most likely to overlook. Help me recognize the beauty of small beginnings and trust the process of your perfect timing. In Jesus' name, Amen.

growing forward

Tending the Soil

What "sticks" in your life have you been tempted to clear away that might actually be the beginning of something beautiful?

In what ways have you seen God working in seemingly insignificant parts of your journey?

How might your perspective change if you looked for potential rather than perfection?

Sowing the Seed

Think about a time when something you initially overlooked or dismissed turned into something valuable. Write down this experience and how it might help you recognize God's work in current "messy" areas of your life. Choose one area where you've been rushing the process and commit to seeing it through God's eyes this week.

Rooting in Truth

"Being confident of this, that he who began a good work in you will carry it on to completion until the day of Christ Jesus." — Philippians 1:6 NIV

Branching Out

Isaiah 43:19, Zechariah 4:10, Matthew 13:31-32

seeds of thought

seeds of thought

i haven't seen beauty
that outshines
crowds of color
than gardens grown
with wild intent
where each bloom
finds its perfect place
nestling in
the field's huddle
to hold the rain's
rooted refreshment
and discover the sway
of the perfect breeze
#barefacedjournals

-day twenty-eight-
growing together

"After this I looked, and there before me was a great multitude that no one could count, from every nation, tribe, people and language, standing before the throne and before the Lamb."
—Revelation 7:9 (NIV)

Have you ever wandered through an English garden? Not the perfectly manicured kind with everything in neat rows, but those magnificent spaces that appear effortlessly wild yet are designed with thoughtful intention? Each plant seems to have found its exact right place—the tall foxgloves standing guard over delicate poppies, climbing roses tangling with clematis, and patches of lavender buzzing with bees. Everything growing together, yet somehow in its own way, creating a tapestry of beauty that could never be achieved through rigid control.

When I met my British husband and lived with his family for the first two years of our marriage in London, these gardens captured my heart.

> *They seemed to whisper a truth about life that I'd been missing—that sometimes the most beautiful things emerge not from our careful planning, but from allowing space for the unexpected to flourish alongside the familiar.*

I think about my friend Bindu, who I met while working abroad. Transplanted from Burma to the UK at a very

young age, her friendship became the most unexpected
bloom in my life's garden during a season when I felt
utterly out of place as an American girl in a foreign
land. Her home filled with amazing spices, dishes with
names I couldn't pronounce, the beautiful saris hanging
in her closet, the jingle of her bracelets as we cooked
together—all of these became precious gifts that
enriched my life in ways I never could have planned.
God's garden—His kingdom—works much the same
way.

In Revelation, John describes a vision of heaven with
a "great multitude that no one could count, from every
nation, tribe, people and language." This isn't just
diversity for diversity's sake—it's a picture of God's
ultimate design.

> *A magnificent garden where each unique*
> *creation has its place, where differences*
> *don't divide but rather create something*
> *more beautiful together than any could alone.*

I wonder how often we miss this because we're trying
to create perfect rows in our lives instead of embracing
God's wilder beauty.

We compartmentalize our relationships, our
ministries, our communities. We stick with who and
what we know, forgetting that the Master Gardener
specializes in bringing unexpected elements together
and we are so much richer for it.

> *What if the very thing your garden is missing—*
> *the element that would make it truly magnificent—*
> *is something completely different from what*
> *you've been cultivating?*

Maybe it's the elderly neighbor with stories that would
bring wisdom like rich compost to your hurried life.
Perhaps it's the colleague from another culture whose

different perspective could help your ideas bloom in new directions. It might even be the person whose life experiences seem nothing like yours, yet whose presence would create the perfect contrast to highlight your unique gifts.

When I felt like a wildflower in the wrong soil during my time abroad, it was my beautiful Bindu blossom who saw me not as out of place, but as exactly where I belonged.

Through her eyes, I began to see that my "American-ness" wasn't something to minimize but something to share. Our differences created something beautiful together—her showing me how to nice round chapatis and we jointly discovered to my sweet friend's dismay that my US-imported Twinkies contained meat (thus a vegetarian no-no).

We had so much learning and laughing together.
We were different plants growing together,
creating something more beautiful than either
of us could have alone.

Heaven won't be filled with rows of identical flowers. It will be like the most magnificent English garden imaginable—a tapestry of different colors, heights, textures, and fragrances, each one planted with intention, each one essential to the whole.

God is far less interested in our careful categories than we are. Where we see differences that divide, He sees diversity that can create extraordinary beauty when grown together with intention.

So I'm wondering—whose presence might add depth,
texture, color to your life in ways you haven't imagined?

What relationship, if nurtured, might create that perfect English garden effect where wild meets intentional and something breathtaking emerges?

> *The most beautiful gardens embrace the*
> *unexpected. They make room for flowers that*
> *weren't in the original plan. Those random glorious*
> *wildflowers are just what we need to enrich the*
> *greater landscape of our lives.*

May our lives and communities be like those English gardens that captured my heart—places where diversity is celebrated, where the unexpected is welcomed, and where each unique creation finds its perfect place in God's grand design.

Prayer: Father, thank You for the beautiful picture of your kingdom—a diverse multitude from every nation, tribe, people, and language. Forgive me for the times I've tried missed the wild beauty you intended me to invite into my space. Help me see beyond my careful plans to embrace the unexpected relationships and opportunities You're growing in my life. Give me eyes to recognize what—or who—might be missing from my garden. Thank You for being a Master Gardener who creates breathtaking beauty from diverse elements growing together. In Jesus's name, Amen.

growing forward

Tending the Soil
What unexpected relationships have enriched your life in ways you never planned?

Where might you be resisting diversity in your life, ministry, or community?

What new "plant" might God be asking you to make room for in your garden?

Sowing the Seed
Identify one person in your life who seems different from you in significant ways. Make a commitment to learn more about their story this week. What unique beauty might they bring to your garden?

Rooting in Truth
"After this I looked, and there before me was a great multitude that no one could count, from every nation, tribe, people and language, standing before the throne and before the Lamb." — Revelation 7:9 (NIV)

Branching Out
Matthew 13:31-32, 1 Corinthians 12:12-27, Isaiah 55:12-13

seeds of thought

seeds of thought

in secret gardens of the soul
seeds of kindness
find their gentle rooting
in soil we may never touch
yet flowers rise
in distant meadows
tended by the
hands of their Creator
in harvests we've forgotten
yet heaven remembers
#barefacedjournals

-day twenty-nine-
fragrant fields we cannot see

"I planted the seed, Apollos watered it, but God has been making it grow." —1 Corinthians 3:6 (NIV)

Let me tell you about heaven. Everyone talks about mansions and crowns, but me? I want fields. Endless, wildly beautiful fields of flowers. Not pristine manicured gardens, but those gloriously messy meadows where every bloom tells a story of persistence.

I want to walk through heavenly landscapes and see the harvest of all those moments we thought were insignificant. The prayers whispered in dark rooms. The kindnesses nobody noticed. The love that seemed to fall on seemingly barren ground.

> *Harvests aren't always about what we can measure. Sometimes they're about what God is doing in the spaces between our understanding.*

We rarely see the full impact of our love, and won't see until the other side of this life. That's the beautiful mystery of God's work through us.

I think about the text message sent during someone's darkest hour. The cup of coffee shared with a stranger. The prayer whispered in a moment of quiet desperation. The kind word spoken when someone feels unseen. These moments seem so small, so insignificant in the grand scheme of things.

*But what if these are the very moments
God uses to transform lives for eternity?*

We're not called to see the entire picture. We're called
to be faithful. To love. To share truth. To care for others
with the hands and feet of Christ—even when we can't
trace the ripple effects of our obedience.

We might never find out how a single act of kindness
became a turning point in someone's life, a smile that
lifted someone out of despair, a listening ear that
prevented a heart from giving up, or a gentle truth
that planted a seed of hope in a seemingly hopeless
situation.

God is always stirring something beneath the surface.
While we see only the smallest glimpse—a momentary
interaction, a brief conversation—He is weaving
together intricate stories of redemption. Our job isn't to
measure the impact, but to be consistently present. To
love without expectation. To serve without counting the
cost.

*I'm learning that eternity isn't built on
grand gestures, but on faithful moments.*

Those quiet acts of love that seem to disappear into the
void—they're actually seeds planted in the most fertile
ground so Holy Spirit can step in to do what we cannot.

*We are co-creators with God in this mysterious
process. Not because we can see the outcome, but
because we trust His ability to take our small offerings
and turn them into something miraculous.*

Every kind word. Every moment of patience. Every
unexpected grace. These are the building blocks of
eternal impact.

We may never know the full story this side of heaven.

But that's the beauty of faith—trusting that our seemingly insignificant moments are actually profound conduits of God's love, capable of changing lives in ways we cannot comprehend.

Prayer: Father, teach me to trust the harvest I cannot see. Help me be patient in the seasons that look dormant, knowing You're always at work. Make me a perennial of faith—growing deeper, stronger, more resilient with each passing year. In Jesus's name, Amen.

growing forward

Tending the Soil
What acts of faithfulness have you continued despite not seeing immediate results?

How does knowing that God sees and nurtures the seeds you plant change your perspective on seemingly "fruitless" ministry?

When have you unexpectedly discovered that something you did or said years ago made a significant impact on someone's life?

Sowing the Seed
Choose one area where you've felt discouraged by a lack of visible results. This week, commit to one small act of faithfulness in this area without expectation of seeing the outcome. Write a prayer surrendering the results to God, acknowledging His role as the one who "makes it grow."

Rooting in Truth
"I planted the seed, Apollos watered it, but God has been making it grow." — 1 Corinthians 3:6 (NIV)

Branching Out
Galatians 6:9, Hebrews 6:10, Ecclesiastes 11:6

seeds of thought

endurance whispers
through bulbs that remember
every winter's test
every drought's defiance
to bloom anyway
in their steady footing
through the struggle rooting
to become stronger still
#barefacedjournals

-day thirty-
stronger through the seasons

**But those who hope in the Lord will renew
their strength. They will soar on wings like eagles;
they will run and not grow weary, they will walk
and not be faint."** — *Isaiah 40:31 (NIV)*

Some plants are just show-offs. You know the type—
those annuals that bloom spectacularly for a hot minute
and then completely fall apart. Beautiful, but fragile.
One harsh wind and they're done. Gone. No resilience.
But perennials? They're the real MVPs of the plant
world. They know something about surviving that goes
way beyond looking good for a season.

I've been that annual Christian. The one who looks
amazing during after an amazing worship services, who
posts the perfect Scripture during a crisis, who seems
spiritually put-together. But underneath—I'm fragile. I'm
struggling not to wither when I feel constantly under
the foot of life's setbacks

> *But that's not sin, it's the frailness of the human
> condition—God made us to depend soley on Him every
> single moment of every single day.*

Even in this, true strength isn't about looking good for
God. It's about having roots so deep that seasons can't
shake you from Him being the foundation that sustains
your life.

My mental health journey taught me this. There were

seasons so dark I thought I'd never bloom again. Seasons where getting out of bed felt like running a marathon. But those roots? They were holding onto something bigger than my desperation.

> *We're not meant to just survive our seasons.*
> *We're meant to become stronger through them.*

Think about how a tree grows. Each ring represents a season—some of abundance, some of incredible challenge. But those rings don't weaken the tree. They become part of its strength. Every difficult season is just another layer of resilience.

> *Our heavenly home won't be all about shiny*
> *crowns or based on perfect performance records.*
> *It will be about the stories of endurance.*

The quiet moments of choosing hope when everything said to give up. The persistent love of the Father that kept showing up, season after season, just because He cares about His children much more than we know.

And every time we choose to keep going, to keep believing, to keep tending the unseen roots, we help make heaven larger—giving Him all the glory.

Prayer: Father, make me strong like a perennial. Not flashy, but faithful. Not perfect, but persistent. Help me trust that every season—even the hard ones—is part of Your cultivation of something beautiful in me. In Jesus's name, Amen.

growing forward

Tending the Soil
What season are you currently walking through?

How have past challenges actually made you stronger?

Where do you need to stop trying to look good and start developing deeper roots?

Sowing the Seed
Take a walk and find a tree or plant that has survived multiple seasons. Reflect on its resilience and ask God to build similar strength in you.

Rooting in Truth
But those who hope in the Lord will renew their strength. They will soar on wings like eagles; they will run and not grow weary, they will walk and not be faint.
— Isaiah 40:31 (NIV)

Branching Out
James 1:2-4, Romans 5:3-5, 2 Corinthians 12:9-10

seeds of thought

seeds of thought

learn to appreciate the life
right in front of your face
in every inch of quiet space
in every giggle
set your mind solid
to circle thankful
for what you have
and your have-nots
for lack is blind to itself
until it is measured by
greener fields and
greater expectations
in a day's ripe harvest
every goodness is on the table
if we'd only open our eyes
on each new sunrise to pay
love forward and
feast on the riches
#barefacedjournals

-a final word-
the garden we're becoming

Congratulations for staying with me for 30 days, and thank you for joining this journey of resistance and resilient persistence. These pages weren't meant to be a roadmap. They are simply heartfelt conversations that I—a barefacedgirl—have had with the Father who loves me, in an attempt to dig into a deeper understanding of His heart.

These conversations continue to build my life's story—messy, beautiful collection of moments where light breaks through—not because darkness is weak, but because relentless faith directs my vision up, no matter how buried I feel. By writing these reflections down, I'm praying you'll see His heart for you, too.

Each reflection is a seed. Some planted intentionally. Some scattered by wind. Some dropped accidentally. But all carrying the potential for something extraordinary.

I still have seasons that feel more like graveyards than gardens. Disappointments that threatened to root me in bitterness. Moments when I feel like giving up looks like the only reasonable option.

But here's what I've learned: We are not defined by our most difficult moments. We are refined by our capacity to keep reaching. And I'm determined to keep looking up, no matter how much my feelings and circumstances fight against me.

Life isn't about avoiding the cracks. It's about finding beauty in unexpected places. About discovering that the very things meant to stop us can become the ground from which we grow most brilliantly.

Some of the most beautiful blooms emerge from the most unlikely soil. Wildflowers don't ask permission. They don't wait for perfect conditions. They simply understand their fundamental purpose: to grow. To reach. To transform whatever landscape they inhabit.

When we started this journey together, we talked about being human in a world that often demands perfection. We explored the tension between cultivating growth and embracing the wild, untamed beauty of who we actually are.

Maybe you've questioned whether anything beautiful could ever emerge from the particular soil where life has planted you. Whether your unique combination of struggles and strengths could possibly produce something worth noticing.

I've wondered if the garden of my life would ever truly flourish or if I'd always be fighting stubborn weeds. And the answer, I've discovered, just like gardening is that both are always happening at once.

But somewhere along the way, I discovered something transformative: The most resilient gardens aren't the perfectly manicured ones. They're the ones that have weathered storms and still found ways to bloom. They're the ones where wilderness and intention dance together in beautiful, unexpected ways.

Your journey won't look like anyone else's. Your garden will grow at its own pace, in its own season. The blooms that eventually emerge might surprise even you.

But know this: God doesn't make mistakes.

*Not in nature. Not in you. Not in the particular mix
of soil and circumstances where He's planted you.*

Your story isn't finished. Not by a long shot.

This book? It's just a glimpse. A snapshot of a journey
still unfolding. An invitation to see yourself the way
God sees you—not as a collection of struggles, but as a
persistent, beautiful becoming.

We are all walking, breathing miracles. Gardens in
progress. Seeds of hope scattered across landscapes of
uncertainty.

Listen closely, and you might hear the whisper of
possibility. It sounds like patience. It feels like hope.
It moves like roots breaking through seemingly
impenetrable ground, drawing life from places others
would have abandoned.

*Because that's what we do. We find a way.
Always. We keep growing, keep blooming, keep
transforming—sometimes despite ourselves,
sometimes because of who we truly are.*

And in the end, maybe that's the most beautiful part
of our story. Not that we've arrived at some perfect
destination, but that we're still becoming. Still
unfolding. Still discovering new depths and dimensions
to the gardens God is growing within us.

May you walk away from these pages with renewed
hope for the wilderness places in your own life. May you
find courage to tend what seems impossible to grow.
And may you rest in the knowledge that the Master
Gardener is still at work, creating beauty in ways
beyond our imagining.

*The light always finds a way through—
                    and so will you—His beautiful flower.*

-more titles from amber-

Leading Ladies:
Discover Your God-Grown Strategy for Success
with Lisa Burris Burns
Multi-award winner & Amazon #1 Bestseller
Discover how life's challenges and triumphs
have shaped ordinary women into extraordinary
influencers for God's Kingdom.
*2nd Edition coming Summer 2025
from Kaleidoscope Publishers*

Leading Ladies: Discovery & Next Steps Journal
with Lisa Burris Burns
Turn inspiration into action with guided reflection to
help you recognize how your journey has
prepared you for influence.
*2nd Edition coming Summer 2025
from Kaleidoscope Publishers*

#sisterhoodoftheshortyellowpencils
Mental Health Mayhem, One Post-It At a Time
Mental health mayhem meets holy hilarity in this
journey from psychiatric ward pencil stubs
to divine revelations.
Coming Spring 2026 from Abundance Books

Leading Hearts Magazine
Free award-winning digital publication empowering
Christian women with authentic voices and practical
leadership resources.
Available at leadinghearts.com

REAL LIFE.
REAL INFLUENCE.
NO MAKEUP REQUIRED.

COFFEE CHAT
with Amber & Lisa

@COFFEECHATLADIES
WWW.COFFEECHATLADIES.COM

Join Amber and her **Leading Ladies** co-author in crime Lisa Burris Burns for candid conversations over coffee. Twice a month, we delve into what it truly means to be a woman of influence in the everyday life—the raw, the good, the bad, and the ugly. Grab your coffee and twist up that messy bun as we chat about the triumphs and trials that shape us and laughter and unfiltered conversations together. Tune in to gain insight and encouragement as we break free from limitations, becoming the world-changing women God created us to be.

No makeup, no pretense required.

Like, subscribe, and download
Coffee Chat with Amber & Lisa—
available on all podcast platforms
including Amazon.

Subscribe to **Coffee Chat Ladies** on YouTube
or **Leading Ladies Life** on the Faithia App.

Visit **www.coffeechatladies.com** for
empowering blog content.

Follow **@coffeechatladies** on
social media for updates and inspiration.

www.ingramcontent.com/pod-product-compliance
Lightning Source LLC
Jackson TN
JSHW011856110525
84225JS00015B/16